D0463836

The Book of Duels

A Duel in Tothill Fields

From an engraving by Cruikshank

(*Mansell Collection*)

The Book of Duels

by

Philip Rush

*With half-tone illustrations
and with drawings by Peter Rush*

GEORGE G. HARRAP & CO. LTD
London   Toronto   Wellington   Sydney

By the same author

Non-Fiction
LONDON'S WONDERFUL BRIDGE
STRANGE PEOPLE
MORE STRANGE PEOPLE
STRANGE STUARTS
HOW ROADS HAVE GROWN
GREAT MEN OF SUSSEX

Fiction
HE WENT WITH DAMPIER
HE WENT WITH FRANKLIN
A CAGE OF FALCONS
THE MINSTREL KNIGHT
APPRENTICE AT ARMS
MY BROTHER LAMBERT
THE CASTLE AND THE HARP

First published in Great Britain 1964
by GEORGE G. HARRAP & Co. LTD
182 High Holborn, W.C.1

© *Philip Rush* 1964

*Composed in Garamond type
and printed by The Whitefriars Press Limited
Made in Great Britain*

Contents

Part 3 : THE DUEL OF HONOUR

Part 4 : DUELLING IN THE UNITED STATES OF AMERICA

Illustrations

INTRODUCTION

It often seems that the sillier a human custom is the longer it lasts.

One man does another an injury, or he insults him, or they fall into heated argument. For many hundreds of years it was the custom for the two to fight a duel with selected weapons to 'settle the matter.' Indeed, the custom still survives among schoolboys and some men, who now fight such 'duels' with their fists.

But what does a duel decide? Only which man can better handle a sword or a pistol or his fists. The injured man, the insulted man, will be killed or beaten if he happens not to shoot or fence or box better. 'Right' triumphs only by accident, and no argument can ever be reasonably settled by a duel.

As Benjamin Franklin, the American statesman and philosopher, said: " It is astonishing that the murderous practice of duelling should continue so long. . . . A man says something which another man tells him is a lie. They fight—but whichever is killed, the point remains unsettled. . . ."

St Foix, a French gentleman put the point still more plainly while sitting in an eighteenth-century coffee-house.

St Foix asked the gentleman next to him to sit farther away.

" Why so, sir? " the gentleman asked.

" Because, sir, you smell."

" That, sir, is an insult. My seconds will wait on you, and you must fight me."

" I will fight if you insist, but I don't see how that will mend the matter," St Foix answered. " If you kill me I shall smell too. If I kill you you will smell, if possible, worse than you do at present."

Yet this simple truth about duelling was not generally understood for many centuries, during which duelling seemed to be regarded as a sacred method of settling a dispute between individuals, much as war has been regarded as a sacred method of settling disputes between nations. In both cases anybody who queried the necessity or the justice of the method was called an unbeliever or a coward.

Duels can conveniently be divided into three kinds:

1. The trial by combat.
2. The duel of chivalry, or treason-duel.
3. The duel of honour.

They came historically in that order, and as one declined, so the next one gained favour and eventually took its place.

I

ORIGIN AND HISTORY

(a) ORIGIN

When we speak of trial by combat we mean a legal trial which was decided by the result of a fight between the accused man and his accuser, not by a judge or a jury.

It was a system unknown to the Greeks or the Romans, and is believed to have been used first by the savage Gothic tribes which overran the mighty Roman Empire. The ancient Egyptians do not mention it, and although we all know how David with his sling slew the mighty Goliath, that was only a pre-battle challenge given in a spirit of vainglory, not a substitute for battle. Trial by combat did not come to the Eastern nations until it was introduced by the Crusaders from Europe, and it was not until 1098 that Kerbogha, the Emir of Mosul, offered to decide his quarrel with the Crusaders by a combat of five or ten champions in place of a battle.

The early Christian Church officially frowned on trial by combat. Gundobad, King of Burgundy, used trial by combat as a legal method in the year 501. This he did because many people were ready to risk their souls by lying, or committing perjury, on oath in a court of law. Gundobad believed that people should put their bodies in danger as well as their souls, and he argued that nobody would be eager to make false accusations if he knew that his life would be endangered.

That might seem good sense, but the method must have had the opposite effect. If a man was a good fighter and knew that the man he disliked was not so good, then he would be more likely to commit perjury. Likewise, anybody who was physically weak would hesitate to tell the truth if he knew that he would have to fight a duel.

Gundobad's Argument

When a bishop protested Gundobad said, " Does not God decide the outcome of both national wars and private fights? If He is a just God, will He not award victory to the righteous cause? "

Single Combat decided by the Judgment of God
From a fifteenth-century French manuscript
(Mansell Collection)

2

The argument for trial by combat has always been based on this belief. In fact, there is a basis of common sense in the argument, so long as you believe that God is just and all-powerful and that His intentions are understood by men.

In those days all men believed that a just, all-powerful God watched over every little happening, even the death of a sparrow. Therefore it seemed reasonable to them for a court of law to say, " O Lord God, here are two men, accuser and accused. We can't decide which one is guilty. If we let them fight, will you give victory to the one whose cause is righteous? "

It never occurred to anybody to ask, " Why fight at all? " If the names of the accused and the accuser had been written on two pieces of parchment thrown from a height, could not God easily have allowed the name of the man speaking the truth to reach the ground first?

But a fight has always attracted; men have always believed that a fight must mean something. In a very short time after Gundobad's law was passed the judicial duel was written into almost every legal system in the countries of Western Europe.

(b) TRIAL BY COMBAT IN ENGLAND

But England in Anglo-Saxon times, after the Romans had gone, retained few connexions with Europe, and it is unlikely that the method of trial by combat reached these shores until we were forcibly linked with Europe by the Norman Conquest of 1066. Then Duke William of Normandy (King William I of England) made it a law of the land.

Trial by Jury

Trial by jury has become so commonplace with us that it is hard to understand that nobody in England was tried by jury until 1164. In fact, trial by jury came in by the back door during the reign of Henry II (1154–89). Henry introduced a procedure by which a man could be accused, or 'indicted,' of a certain crime by a sworn body of neighbours. This was in place of having one accuser, or 'appealer.'

The accused was tried by ordeal or by combat as before. But gradually he was allowed to "put himself upon his country for good or ill"—that is, another body, or jury, of sworn neighbours would decide whether he was guilty or not. This sort of jury had first been used to decide whether a man was fit enough to endure trial by combat.

Trial by combat had taken the place of trial by ordeal as time went on, and the ordeal was officially abolished under Henry III in 1218. In trial by ordeal, as the name implies, innocence was proved if the accused came through an ordeal relatively unharmed. For instance, if he (or she) did not sink when flung inside a sack into water, or was able to carry a red-hot piece of iron a certain distance, this was accepted as proof of innocence. Now trial by combat was gradually being replaced by trial by jury. The custom grew of allowing the accused to decline trial by combat and to "put himself upon his neighbours."

Trial by Combat still in Force

It should be remembered, however, that for a long time trial by jury was only an alternative to trial by combat. The accused could still choose to fight, and obviously he would so choose when he thought he had a good chance of winning. The choice was gradually whittled down until trial by combat could take place only in cases of treason or murder. The legal right to choose trial by combat did not, in fact, disappear from English law until modern times.

In 1818 a man named Thornton was accused of murder, and as he was almost certainly guilty his clever lawyer advised him to plead " Not guilty " and add, " I am ready to defend the same by my body."

Now, trial by combat had not been used for centuries, but the law had never been repealed.

Thornton was given a pair of gloves. He wore one, and the other was thrown down in the ancient and approved manner, being taken into the custody of the court as a wager of battle. Nobody present would ' take up his glove,' nobody would ' wage battel ' with the accused, and the Court of Appeal decided in Thornton's favour. The judges said, " The law of the land allows trial by combat, and it is our duty to pronounce the law as it is, not as we would wish it to be. . . ."

As a result of his lawyer's cunning, Thornton was discharged. But Parliament hastened to abolish trial by combat before anybody could work off old grudges. On March 22, 1819, this alleged pillar of the Constitution was abolished for good, and nobody appeared to be any the worse.

How Trial by Combat Worked

In Europe various methods of fighting a trial by combat were practised. Sometimes the combatants fought barefoot and bareheaded, with sword and shield. Or they might use clubs or batons. But after the tenth century clubs were used only by base-born men, and all men of gentle birth fought with shield and lance, sword and helmet.

When it was a matter of life and death a bier stood by, draped in black, ready to carry away the body of the man who lost. If not killed in the fight, he was immediately executed.

The first recorded duel on horseback took place in A.D. 880.

But there were amusing variations—at least, the spectators of those days found them amusing. For example, in Germany if a woman accused a man of breach of promise to marry, or if a husband and a wife disagreed, the matter was settled by a fight between man and woman.

The gentleman's left arm was tied to his side, and he was placed in a tub sunk waist-deep in the ground. His only weapon was a short baton in his right hand. The lady was provided with a heavy stone sewn up in the lengthened sleeve of the solitary undergarment she was allowed to wear.

The lady could circle round the tub and await her chance to settle the argument with her stone—a crushing argument, in fact. The gentleman was badly handicapped, like modern men batting left-handed or with broomsticks against women at cricket—but the lady did not always win. An ancient picture shows the lady in one of these combats with her head in the tub and her heels in the air!

Another curious custom grew up among the Norsemen. Right of appeal after a duel was lost if the victor, with a single blow, could kill an unfortunate bull produced for the purpose.

The Legal Procedure

In England the legal procedure was for the accuser to ' appeal ' the accused of the crime, state the facts, and offer to prove it by his body. The defender had to deny the whole accusation, word for word, and offer to prove his innocence by his body.

Each champion, with his coat undone, his head shaven, his legs and arms bare, had to kneel and hand his glove, with a penny in each finger, to the judge. Then the two men had to go to two separate churches and " offer there the five pennies which were in their gloves, to honour the five wounds of God so that God might give the victory to him who was in the right."

When the judge had decided that a duel would be proper the parties also had to find ' weds,' or pledges— that is, neighbours who would go bail for their due appearance on the day of battle.

The judge then said, somewhat unnecessarily, " Let them come armed," and named the day.

The Actual Fight. It was fought in a levelled and prepared piece of ground, usually sixty feet square, enclosed with pales and having seats for the judges of the Court of Common Pleas and the Law Serjeants.

The champions were introduced by two knights, and were sometimes dressed in coats of armour, with red sandals, bare-legged from the knees downward, bareheaded, and with bare arms to the elbows. But as time passed these details were not always insisted upon.

The combatants took various oaths, including one against sorcery and enchantment, which ran roughly as follows:

> Hear this, ye justices, that I have neither eaten, drunk, nor have I upon me either bone, stone, or grass; no enchantment, sorcery, or witchcraft; whereby the law of God may be abased, or the law of the Devil exalted. So help me, God and his Saints!

The battle then started, the defendant or his champion fighting from the north and the accuser or his champion from the south.

The men had to fight until the stars appeared in the evening, and if the defendant held out until then he was not guilty. But if either man was killed or forced to yield, confessing himself 'craven,' the day was, of course, immediately lost. 'Craven' did not originally mean cowardly, but was a general admission of disgrace.

In civil cases the beaten man not only lost the case, he 'lost his law' (or reputation as an honest man), because the result of the fight showed that he had been lying. As an infamous and degraded person, he could never be heard as a witness again.

In criminal cases of murder, homicide, theft, etc., the accused, if defeated, lost not only his life but his property. If, however, the accuser was beaten the punishment varied. Sometimes he was executed, but more often he was imprisoned or mutilated or fined for making a false charge.

Revenue from Trials by Combat

In fact, although trials by combat cost money, they brought in valuable revenue to the king and others. Once a battle was pledged it could not be called off except by payment of a heavy fine to the judge as a ' concord.' If either champion failed to appear another heavy fine became payable as a ' recreancy.'

In King Stephen's time (1135–54) a certain man owed the Crown one hundred measures of wine for the ' concord ' of his brother's duel. Large fines were paid to Henry II for recreancy, for refusal to fight, and for irregularities in procedure.

Fines were paid in money and in horses for not keeping the record of a duel, for fighting a duel in the ' hundred ' court when it should have been fought before the sheriff in his court, for duelling in the king's court, for ' appealing ' the theft of a cow in a court which had no right to try the case. A man certainly needed a good lawyer in those days, and it becomes plain why so many gentlemen studied the law when they had no intention of practising as lawyers.

One lady had to pay a fine because she had agreed to fight her brother in a duel and then had decided that blood was thicker than water. Not unreasonably, another man had to pay a heavy fine because, after confessing to King Richard I (1189–99) that he had no right to certain lands, he had the impudence to wage battle for them. This was one man who evidently did not believe that God would point out the guilty party.

Not all revenues went to the Crown. Henry I gave the jurisdiction of duels to a church of St Peter. This church ordered that the victor in a duel must offer thanks to St Peter for his victory and give the arms of the vanquished man to St Peter's Church as a sign of gratitude.

A record of the twelfth year of Henry II's reign (1166)

shows that Henry paid out in the year £9 11s. 3d. to cover the expenses of 34 trials by ordeal, 14 defacements, 14 hangings, and 5 trials by combat. But the duel was also used as an instrument of justice in three courts—county court, hundred court, and baron's court—and the King's income and the income of those lords who had custom of pit and gallows must have shown a clear profit from fines over expenditure.

The Approver

The so-called 'approver' of the twelfth and thirteenth centuries would nowadays be dubbed an informer—a criminal who turns king's evidence, or a 'grass.' The difference was that the approver had to prove the truth of what he said by fighting the men he accused.

Most prosecutions in those rough days needed a private accuser to appear in court, but people hesitated to give evidence, knowing that they would have to fight if the accused man chose, and that, if they lost, they would be liable to imprisonment or a fine.

Therefore the Crown got hold of one of the lesser criminals whenever it could and invited him to turn approver or informer against his fellow-criminals. He would usually agree in the hope of saving his own life.

This may have been necessary, up to a point, when there was no police system to detect criminals. But it led to false accusations, made out of spite or to gain money or a pardon. The Crown often kept an approver in prison and made him fight five trials by combat, putting him up to accuse the men the Crown wanted to accuse, whether he knew anything of the matter or not.

This obviously brought the law into disrepute, and the Crown did not always play fair with the approver, having been known to hang him even when he had been five times victorious. This was a pretty scurvy trick even for those days, and a lawyer of the times said, in a tone of faint irritation, that when an approver had done what he said he would do or what he was asked to do, faith should be kept with him.

Hired Champions

But it was not only the Crown that made money through fines from trials by combat. There arose a class of professional champion who fought for hire and made a good thing out of it.

In theory, the accused and the accuser had to fight in person. With few exceptions no substitutes were allowed. Even priests had to fight in person until 1176, when Henry II first excused a priest from the trial by combat, saying that priests could not be expected to fight duels.

Women were exempt, and men over sixty if they so desired. Men who pleaded ' mayhem '—that is, inability to fight because of broken bones or the loss of an ear, a nose, or an eye—were also exempt, but only if the judge allowed the plea. It was even held that broken front teeth qualified for mayhem, as " strong front teeth help greatly to victory." That certainly makes one wonder about the gentlemanliness of these legal fights, a doubt fully borne out by the description of the duel between Thomas Whithorn and James Fisher in 1456, described later in this book.

So these hired champions were not officially approved, and any champion who did take another man's place was supposed to have been a witness of the offence. That is why, if he lost, the punishment was heavy. Had not God pointed him out as a liar on oath? In Europe a defeated champion had his hand cut off. In England the law was not so harsh, preferring fines as a rule.

But if a man was caught acting as a hired champion for an act he knew nothing about and had not witnessed, then indeed the law was harsh.

In about 1220 Elias Piggun appeared to vouch for a stolen mare. His opponent in court said that Piggun was a hired champion who had been paid to appear, and that he knew nothing of the truth of the matter. Elias had to admit that he was a teacher of sword-play, and the jury found him guilty of fraud. Poor Piggun was sentenced to lose a foot, and was told that he was lucky to get off so lightly.

But despite these dangers and the hazards of the fight, championship became a regular occupation, and the surname Champion, as a result, was quite a common one. No doubt it was often difficult to prove that a champion had not witnessed the crime, if he had been well primed with the facts.

After 1176 clergymen used hired champions openly, which was perhaps reasonable, as they were not expected to fight themselves.

One example of a churchman using a champion concerns, amazingly enough, one William Piggun, brother to Elias Piggun, the hired champion already mentioned as having lost a foot. The Pigguns were evidently a large, self-confident, and fighting family, for William took on the job of championing Ralph Gubuin, Prior of Tynemouth, in a dispute with Simon of Tynemouth.

William Piggun was a *magnus pugil*, a great champion, and the innocent monks were gleefully confident of victory. But, alas! their chronicler ruefully records that " our great champion was vanquished, and Simon, our adversary, won his case."

The Shaving of Champions. It was the custom for a champion before fighting to have the hair of his head shaved off. The origin of this is unknown, but that it was so is shown by King Richard I, Richard Lionheart. In 1190, setting sail on his Crusade, Richard ordered that any seaman convicted of theft was to be tarred and feathered and set ashore when the ship touched land, but first he was to be " shaved after the fashion of a champion."

By the end of the thirteenth century, however, the pretence that a champion could not be hired was dropped. From then on a man openly hired a champion to fight in his place. Naturally he would choose the best champion he could afford, as a man later came to hire the best lawyer he could afford.

2

SOME HISTORIC TRIALS BY COMBAT

BEFORE 1066

The Norse sagas speak of the judicial combat, and in those early days a man's whole property might be staked on the issue. Therefore a skilful fighter could earn a good living, and in the tenth century Liot the Pale, a wandering Scotsman of huge physique, busied himself in Norway in " the rite and rigour of single combat," and soon became rich. Champions took themselves so seriously that they were often teetotallers, an extraordinary thing for those hard-drinking days. Perhaps Liot the Pale forgot this rule when he came up against the famous Norse warrior, champion-killer, and poet, Egill Skallagrímsson. Skalla-grímsson beat Liot in a duel about an heiress, and so " vindicated all his goods to himself according to law. . . ."

The Chevalier Gontran and Count Ingelger (880)

But these were rude times in which it is difficult to make sure which is fact and which is legend. It does seem, however, that the first trial by combat recorded was fought on horseback, and took place in France in 880.

The Count of Gastonois had been found dead in bed with his wife. Gontran, a cousin of the dead man, accused the Countess of Gastonois of her husband's murder.

The King of France appointed a day for a trial by combat at the Castle of Landon.

Now, Gontran was the most expert and experienced swordsman in France, perhaps in the whole world, and everybody was horrified when Ingelger, Count of Anjou, godson of the Countess of Gastonois, a charming boy not yet sixteen years of age, threw himself at the King's feet.

" My liege lord, permit me to defend my godmother against this foul accusation."

The King smiled and patted the boy's head. " Ingelger, you are brave, but it would mean certain death. The name of Gontran strikes terror into the bravest man. You have no experience, but Gontran has won more duels than anybody can count."

" My lord, I am unworthy of so great an honour, but I wish to put the matter in God's hands," the boy Count answered firmly.

It seems that the boy was the only one who thought that God gave victory to the just cause, or else that the King believed the Countess to be guilty. The King was much troubled, and the courtiers tried to dissuade Ingelger, but nothing would move him. The King had to give permission, and the cry went up: " Alas! that so promising a boy should destroy himself! "

In fact, in those days it was not extraordinary to fight in battle or in duels at sixteen years of age. Men were knighted and married and generally considered adult at that age. But Ingelger had always been in delicate health and had taken no part in battle or the rough sports of the times.

On the appointed day the young Count cheerfully took

leave of his weeping godmother, the Countess of Gastonois, assuring her that God would clear her name. Ingelger made his confession and heard Mass in the chapel of the Castle of Landon. Then he distributed alms to the poor and mounted his war-charger. When Ingelger entered the lists a great sigh arose from the assembled company. The boy looked so frail, perched on his huge horse, whereas Gontran seemed too big for his horse.

The Countess of Gastonois and Gontran both affirmed on oath the truth of what they had said, and swore that they had not used black magic in preparation for the coming fight. The judges solemnly announced that the matter would be put to the test.

The trumpets sounded and the combatants carefully placed their lances in rest. Then the snorting horses thundered down on each other, and there came a tremendous crash. Gontran had thrust at young Ingelger's shield, but the boy calmly turned the blow, and his own lance pierced Gontran's eye and passed into his brain.

A cry of joy echoed round the castle as Ingelger jumped down to cut off Gontran's head and display it to the King as undeniable proof that God had spoken and pointed to his godmother as the innocent party.

The Countess of Gastonois, as a reward for his bravery or his belief in God's justice, presented Ingelger with the manor of Landon, including the castle. The young Count would later be able to point out to his children the exact spot where he had killed the renowned champion when still only an inexperienced boy, and no doubt as he grew older he overdid the telling, and his children grew bored with even that brave story!

King Cnut and King Edmund (1016)

There is an account of the peace of 1016 between the Danish King Cnut and the English King Edmund which says that they fought a duel for England on the Isle of Alney, near Gloucester.

At the start Cnut pressed Edmund hard, who, we are told, was " stout and broad "—that is to say, rather fat. During a pause the Dane said, " Edmund, you are panting far too much."

Edmund made no answer, only blushing fiery red, but when the fight started again Edmund dealt Cnut such a blow that he went sprawling on hands and knees. Edmund did not try to kill Cnut, but held back and said, " I don't pant too much for one who lays so mighty a king at his feet."

When the Danes saw this they were happy to make peace, and the two kings divided England between them.

Whether this episode ranks as exact history is doubtful, but it certainly makes a good story.

BETWEEN 1066 AND 1300

If you were an Englishman accused by a Norman of murder, lying in court, manslaughter, or open robbery, you had the choice of defending yourself at a trial by ordeal or a trial by combat. That is, you could carry a chunk of red-hot iron and prove your innocence by not taking much hurt. If you were badly burned you did not have to worry about the pain for long, because you were quickly put out of your misery. You were executed.

Or you could fight your accuser in a trial by combat. If you had to admit defeat you were guilty and, again, put to death without delay. If you won or kept fighting all day until sunset you were innocent and your accuser suffered death or disablement.

If you happened to be a Norman you had the same choice as the Englishman. But you had one advantage in that you could clear yourself if you found enough witnesses to swear on oath that you were innocent. That was not done to put the Normans 'one up' on the English, but because it was a custom in Normandy, and so it was only fair that it should apply to Normans over here.

Therefore an Englishman who refused to fight must go to the ordeal or confess himself guilty. But a Norman who would not fight or go to the ordeal might still clear himself by the oaths of witnesses.

By 1086 trial by combat was well established here, and it applied to civil actions as well as to criminal. If you claimed a piece of land or a right of way from your neighbour you could prove you were right by fighting and beating him.

William of Eu (1096)

In 1096 William of Eu was charged with treason and defeated in the trial by combat that followed. As punishment, in the savage manner of those times, William was blinded, because the laws of William the Conqueror said that the mutilated body should remain as evidence of treason, and no doubt as a living warning to others.

Ordgar and Edgar the Atheling (about 1096)

At about the same time an Englishman named Ordgar wished to curry favour with William II, William Rufus, son of William the Conqueror. He accordingly accused

18

Edgar the Atheling of saying that he and his children were the rightful heirs to the Crown. The case was ordered to be tried by combat, but as Edgar was advanced in years, an Englishman named Godwine of Winchester fought in his place.

" And when silence had been proclaimed by a herald, the gages of both were thrown into the place of combat by the judge, who cried aloud that God, who knows all secrets, would declare the truth of this cause."

There was a fierce fight. When Godwine had nearly won his sword broke from its hilt and he was in sore trouble. But as Ordgar triumphantly pressed him Godwine managed to pick up his blade, and, grasping it with two fingers (the chronicler says " delicately," but a better word would have been " miraculously "), he pierced Ordgar in the eye and felled him. But when Godwine set his foot on his fallen opponent Ordgar's treachery became obvious to all. He had sworn to carry no weapons except those of a knight, but he drew a dagger from his boot and tried to stab Godwine. The dagger was wrenched away, and Ordgar then confessed that his charge against Edgar had been false. But his confession did him no good: he was stabbed again and again until " the deep wounds drove out his ungodly soul."

Baron Henry de Essex and Robert de Montford (1163)

A famous combat took place in 1163. In the Welsh expedition of 1157, Henry of Essex fought at the side of King Henry II, as befitted the Constable and royal standard-bearer of England. But at a critical moment Essex threw down his banner and cried out that the King was slain. This may have been panic, it may have been deliberate treachery, but whatever it was it nearly brought about the defeat of the English army, which was in a dangerous pass in the Welsh mountains.

The mutterings against the Constable grew in volume until, in 1163, Robert de Montford in Parliament 'appealed' him of treason and a trial by combat was decided upon.

They met at Reading and fought on an island in the Thames near the Abbey. Essex was beaten, but he produced something new in excuses for losing a fight. He declared that when the combat was at its height he saw the glorious king and martyr, Edmund, complete in armour, hovering in the air and frowning at him, full of righteous anger. And by the side of the wrathful saint Henry saw a knight he himself had murdered. This so unnerved him, he declared, that he made a rash attack on de Montford and was struck down.

He was thought to be dead, and the body was given to the monks of Reading for burial. The monks discovered life still in Baron Henry de Essex. He recovered and, by the King's grace, was allowed to turn monk himself. It was in the Abbey of Reading, to Samson, later Abbot of St Edmund's, that Henry told his story of how he had come to lose the trial by combat.

There is no doubt that such a ghost would hinder fair play, although it could be argued that God must have known all about the ghost's appearance. But when a trial by combat was in progress it was an offence to speak or do anything to interfere. In 1213, for example, Roger de Parles incurred a sentence of banishment for aiding his brother Henry in a duel at Tothill, in London, though King John, in one of his rare moments of forgiveness, later pardoned him.

Hugh Bolare and William the Long (1292)

These trials by combat were not confined to the aristocracy. In 1292, at the Manor of Glassonby, a countryman called William the Long heard Hugh Bolare say that he, William the Long, had received an ox stolen from a man named Gilbert the Goose. William was so indignant that he immediately offered to prove on his body that Hugh was lying.

" Whereupon it was, by the judgment of the court, decided that there should be a duel betwixt them, which duel was waged, armed and fought between them in such wise that the foresaid Hugh, vanquished in the duel, was, by the judgment of the court, hanged."

This was in the baronial court at Carlisle, and there was some argument as to whether it should have been tried there, but that was too late to help Hugh Bolare.

(*c*) BETWEEN 1300 AND 1400

The Prior of Tynemouth's Champion (1346)

During the reign of Edward III, in 1346, the priory of Tynemouth was again in trouble. The priory owned the manor of Hawkslaw, but a dangerous neighbour, Gerard de Widdrington, son of a border family well known in song and story, also claimed it.

Gerard de Widdrington made himself very unpleasant, and the monks of Tynemouth went in bodily fear. Widdrington tried to kill the Prior, and seized and tortured some Dominican friars in the mistaken belief that his victims were monks of the priory.

The chronicler tells us that the Prior had a " nose delicately aquiline," which seems somewhat beside the point until you realize that there was a literary convention which regarded an aquiline nose as evidence of high birth. The Prior's noble friends included a lady of the house of Percy, who sent him jewels to defray the legal costs. Even more important, she sent him a knight, Sir Thomas Colville.

Now, Sir Thomas Colville had a great reputation because of an exploit he had performed in France. A French knight on the far bank of a river boasted that nobody in the English army dared cross to fight him. Colville was the only one to accept the challenge. He set spurs to his horse, swam the stream, and reached the bank in safety. Then he charged the Frenchman, pierced him like a chicken on a spit, and swam back. Nowadays he would doubtless have come back to find himself famous, and would have appeared on television.

But even in those days, when news had to travel by pedlar or pilgrim, Colville's fame was enough. When he stood forth to champion the Prior's cause nobody dared fight him. Gerard de Widdrington remembered other engagements and disappeared.

"Wherefore, the Prior's adversaries losing heart, he gained the wished-for termination of the aforesaid suit," the monkish chronicler blithely recorded.

Sir John de Visconti and Sir Thomas de la Marche (1350)

On October 4, 1350, a famous duel took place in England between two foreigners. Sir John de Visconti, a Cypriot, challenged Sir Thomas de la Marche, an illegitimate son of the King of France. Sir John alleged that Sir Thomas had taken bribes and betrayed a Christian army to the Turks.

The duel was fought in England because Edward III's

reputation for valour and chivalry was so high that both combatants chose him as judge of the affair. But this was bitterly resented in France, of which more later.

The battle was fought at Westminster within the boundaries of the King's palace. At the first charge the lances broke against the shields without unhorsing either knight. Alighting, they drew their swords and fought on foot. They fought so long that their swords broke, and then they began to wrestle. The knights wore impenetrable armour, and even the visors of their helmets were guarded with small bars of steel.

But the Frenchman had had the foresight to provide himself with short and sharp points of steel fastened on the knuckles of his right gauntlet, and with these he struck at his opponent's face through the bars of the visor. Poor Sir John could not return the blows, and in this unfortunate and painful situation the Cypriot was forced to yield.

King Edward III threw down his baton, the Marshal cried "Ho!" and the fight ceased. The vanquished knight became the victor's prisoner, but Sir Thomas chivalrously released his captive without ransom and donated his captive's armour to St George's Chapel, in the church of St Paul in London.

The Prince of Wales set the Cypriot free, which was a chivalrous, almost foolish, thing to do if the man were guilty. But the end of the story is far from chivalrous. When the triumphant Sir Thomas de la Marche returned to France, where a jealous brother now reigned, he was beheaded for high treason because he had agreed to fight the trial by combat in the Court of the English King.

Trial by Combat between Man and Dog (1400)

Trials by combat were becoming fewer in this hundred-year period, but the following combat, which took place in 1400, was certainly the most curious of all time. It is so unusual that it is included here, although this book is mainly concerned with duels fought by the English-speaking nations.

In the year 1400 Aubry Montargis, taking a lonely walk near Paris, was murdered and buried under a tree. His dog, left at home, went out at night to search for his master and discovered his grave. The dog ran to the Chevalier Ardilliers, a friend of the dead man, and refused to be quiet until the Chevalier allowed himself to be led to a large oak in the forest. There the dog howled and scratched furiously at the earth. The Chevalier told his servant to dig, and the body of Montargis was found.

Later the dog met his master's murderer and attacked him with such ferocity that it took many men to restrain him. This happened many times, and the faithful dog, usually as quiet as a lamb, turned into a raging tiger every time he saw this man, the Chevalier Maquer.

It was remembered that Maquer had spoken against Montargis, and King Charles was asked to observe the dog's behaviour. This was so extraordinary that the King, although disliking trials by combat, decided that it was a proper method to use in this case. No doubt it seemed to the King that if Maquer could not beat a dog, then a guilty conscience must be paralysing his arm.

All Paris was there to watch the Chevalier Maquer enter the lists with his lance in his hand. The dog was let loose, and a terrific commotion ensued. The dog

threw himself at the man from all directions—he was
like a thing possessed. But no matter how often Maquer
thrust with his lance he could not touch the dog—it was
like fighting a shadow. And the dog was watching for

The Chevalier Maquer cried that he would confess

his chance as coolly as a Roman gladiator; it came when
Maquer stumbled and the point of his lance was lowered.
Like a flash, the dog had him by the throat, and, screaming with fear, the Chevalier Maquer cried that he would
confess if only they would pull the dog away.

The French King was so impressed with this example of canine intuition and faithfulness that he had a marble monument, suitably inscribed, erected on the spot where the murder had been committed.

(d) AFTER 1400

In the fifteenth century trial by combat was indeed nearing its end, but the period is interesting by reason of the last approver's (or professional accuser's) duel.

Thomas Whithorn and James Fisher (1456)

This took place towards the end of the long reign of Henry VI (1422–61). Whithorn, a thief, was imprisoned at Winchester. To save his life he made a series of accusations against honest men, and, as he was successful in the trials that followed, some of the men he accused were hanged.

This went on for three years, and each time Whithorn went back to prison and drew his three halfpence, the daily wage due to a king's approver. Then a meek Londoner, James Fisher, when accused by Whithorn swore that he would " spend his life and his blood to prove that Whithorn was a liar."

The watching crowd did not like approvers, and they also felt that Whithorn would be too strong for James Fisher, the " meek innocent," as he was called. They shouted, " Hang uppe Thomas Whithorn." The judge was inclined to agree with them, but he had to let the fight go on.

Dressed in white sheepskin and carrying strong staves, the two men entered the ground at Winchester. The meek defendant knelt down to pray, but the accuser,

Whithorn, becoming impatient, cried, " You false traitor, why are you so long? " At which the defendant, full of righteous wrath, rose from his knees and smote the approver, but, alas! broke his own weapon. The judge allowed the approver only one stroke at the defendant, and then took his club away also. The two men fought with fists and rested, and fought again and rested. Then, as William Gregory, Mayor of London and recorder of the fight, says, " They went together by the neck."

The men fought with their teeth, so that their coats and their flesh were all " rente," and the end seemed to have come when the false accuser " caste that meek innocent downe to the grownde."

But in this last deadly wrestle, more by luck than judgment, the innocent defender " got up on his knees and took that false approver by the nose with hys teeth and put hys thombe in hys eye so that the approver cried out and prayed for mercy, for he was false unto God and unto hym."

So the trial ended, and the judge pronounced sentence upon the approver, whose fate Gregory piously records: " And then he was confessed and hanged, of whose soul God have mercy. Amen."

The Last Trial by Combat

The last actual trial by combat in Great Britain took place in 1597 in Scotland, when Adam Bruntfield challenged and slew James Carmichael for murdering his brother Steven.

But the fact that trial by combat was no more than a dead letter in England is effectively shown by an Elizabethan scene in 1571.

27

Paramour and his Champion, George Thorne (1571)

In June of that year, the thirteenth of Queen Elizabeth's reign, the legal profession was thrown into confusion by a man named Paramour, who insisted on using trial by combat in a civil case. This concerned the right of some manorial lands in the Isle of Harty, part of the Isle of Sheppey, in Kent.

The lawyers could do no more than allow the legal formalities to be observed. The wager was made by the defendant's champion throwing down his glove, which the other champion took up. Lists of the correct size (sixty feet square) were made ready in Tothill Fields, in London, and scaffolds were set around for the spectators.

The defendant's champion, George Thorne, " a big, broad, strong-set fellow," entered the lists first, and then the plaintiff's champion, " a proper slender man and not so tall as the other," named Henry Nailer, a fencing master, came next, heralded by drum and fife, with Thorne's glove carried in front of him upon a sword's point. The two men were duly apparelled in leather armour, bare-legged, shaven, and bare-armed to the elbow, and they took all the proper oaths.

But the judges knew that the case had been settled because of the intervention of the Queen the day before. The defendant did not appear, and the court gave judgment against him. The Lord Chief Justice ordered Nailer to give Thorne back his glove.

It is perhaps not uncharitable to believe that Nailer had come there merely for self-advertisement in his profession of fencing master. He said that he would not give the glove back willingly without a fight, and suggested that Thorne and he should exchange half a dozen blows to " show some pastime " to the Lord Chief Justice and the four thousand people assembled there. But Thorne had evidently come seriously ready to fight, for he answered surlily that he had come to fight and would not play. Who could blame him? But the Lord Chief Justice pointedly praised Nailer for his valiant courage, and then " commanded them both quietly to depart the field."

Proclamation was then made that everybody should go home, every man in the peace of God and the Queen. The four thousand spectators thereupon meekly dispersed with a shout of " Long live the Queen! "

This is certainly not the sort of behaviour one would expect from Elizabethans deprived of their entertainment, and it is a far cry from the days, 115 years before, when a " meek, innocent defender " could win a fight by fixing his teeth in his opponent's nose and sticking his thumb in his eye.

I

RISE OF THE DUEL OF CHIVALRY IN ENGLAND

(*a*) Decline of Trial by Combat in the Reign of Edward I

An important reason for the decline of the trial by combat was the character of King Edward I (1272–1307).

Edward was a strong, sensible king, a practical man who hated waste. He disliked his subjects to fight trials by combat. If men wanted to fight and kill each other, no matter what the excuse, Edward considered that they would be much better employed fighting in his armies.

But he could not always stop trials by combat, because they were written into the law of the country. In fact, he was himself accused of felony before the Court of France by Gaston of Béarn, a Gascon. The English King had to send five knights across the Channel to accept battle on his behalf, but the accusation was dropped. No doubt the French King did not care for any king to be accused by a subject: such a thing would obviously be dangerous for all kings.

Edward did all he could to discourage such trials, and for the same reason he did not like the duel of chivalry, which was coming into favour from France.

Edward I and the Duel of Chivalry

The duel of chivalry was confined to knights and the upper classes. It was used as a trial in accusations of treason, but it was used also to settle points of honour. A knight might declare that no Frenchman could ride a horse properly, or that all Frenchmen were natural liars, and offer to ' prove ' it by fighting. If a Frenchman took him up, a duel of chivalry followed.

Now, this sort of thing offended Edward I's hatred of waste and his dislike of slovenly thinking. He was too good a statesman to let so-called duels of chivalry have their place in English law, as trials by combat had done. He had more useful work for his knights than to allow them to meet each other, " appareled as knights with knightly arms," for empty points of honour.

A knight called Sir Nicholas de Segrave found to his cost that King Edward meant what he said. During a quarrel with another knight, Sir John de Cromwell, Sir Nicholas challenged him to fight. King Edward refused to allow the fight, and when Sir Nicholas tried to cross the Channel to fight in France he was arrested and promptly condemned to death. This was rough, un-chivalrous conduct on the part of the King, and must have caused a stir in the knightly pavilions. Probably the knights believed that the King was not serious, but the fierce old Plantagenet was in earnest. Sir Nicholas had to talk very fast and declare that it was his extreme anger against Sir John de Cromwell that made him forget his duty to the King, or else he would undoubtedly have been executed.

But even Edward I could not hold out against that greatest waster of all, Death, and his son, Edward II

(1307–27), and his grandson, Edward III (1327–77), were men of very different minds.

(b) THE DUEL OF CHIVALRY IMPORTED FROM FRANCE

These two Edwards were great imitators of things French, and Edward III even claimed the French throne and started the Hundred Years War to secure it. The duel of chivalry was established in England during the long reign of this king.

Edward III was a shrewd man as well as a chivalrous one, and he no doubt realized that the people loved to see the bright armour and the gay trappings of the knights, the horses, and the spectators in a duel of chivalry. But the duel also appealed to Edward as a warrior, and it was he who first gave a semi-legal status to the duel of chivalry.

Edward III challenges King Philip of France (1340)

In 1340 Edward turned from the siege of Tournai to challenge the French King Philip to decide their quarrel by a duel. " To avoid the death of Christians, and as the question concerns us and you alone, the discussion of our challenge should be made between our two bodies." Failing this, Edward suggested that there could be a combat of " a hundred persons, the most sufficient," on either side. But Philip would not agree, and so went on to the national disaster of the battle of Crécy.

A king who was ready to risk himself so gallantly was bound to affect the national outlook. This dashing, chivalrous attitude to life became fashionable for the upper classes to practise and the lower classes to applaud. In fact, it was only outward show: a knight often behaved most chivalrously in the lists and yet would put a whole town to the sword—men, women, and children—without the least compunction.

But the duel of chivalry suited the times perfectly, and it was during the reign of Edward's successor, Richard II (1377–99), son of the Black Prince, that this kind of duel reached its peak.

Richard II challenges King Charles of France (1383)

In fact, intentionally or not, Richard was to repeat Edward III's suggestion that the right to the Crown of France should be decided by combat between the two claimants. Richard, in the seventh year of his reign, on September 8, 1383, while he was still a young man fresh from his personal triumph in Wat Tyler's rebellion, suggested he should fight a duel with Charles VI of France. He was willing to fight singly or to take part in a combat in which each monarch should be accompanied by his three uncles. " To stay the effusion of Christian blood and the desolation of the land " was the reason given in the challenge.

It is certainly a pity that this idea did not catch on. If all wars during the last 580 years had been settled by the opposing kings or statesmen fighting, the millions of lives saved and the human misery avoided would have been incalculable. But Charles VI would have none of it.

The Duel of Chivalry becomes Part of English Law

Richard was still an eager boy when chivalry at last forced its way into English law. In about 1390 his uncle Thomas of Woodstock, the Constable of England, wrote his *Ordinance* setting out elaborate rules to be followed in a duel of chivalry. A Court of Chivalry was later set up in which the Marshal and Constable of England acted as officials both of law and chivalry. This court had the power to try treason by the duel.

The House of Commons quite rightly said that this was an encroachment on the law of the land, but Richard was too dazzled by tournaments and the concept of chivalry to understand that he was treading on dangerous ground.

(c) DECLINE OF CHIVALRY

The custom of fighting duels and tournaments of chivalry did add much to the colour and pageantry of life from the fourteenth to the fifteenth centuries. Towards the end of the fifteenth century chivalry was dying—chivalry, that is, in the sense of knightly chivalry. The knight on horseback was losing his power. He had had to give way to the unmounted archer, as at Crécy and Agincourt, but he could still pretend that things had not changed, that the gentlemen were still in charge of all that was noble in battle.

The coming of gunpowder put an end to such pretence. The knight's power vanished, and even Henry VIII, in his Field of the Cloth of Gold, could not restore the knight's splendour. Once the knight had gone, the duel of chivalry vanished with him, together with all its artificial trappings. The last duel of chivalry in England was fought in 1492.

2

SOME HISTORIC DUELS OF CHIVALRY

Turnebole, his Dog, and Sir Robert de Venale (1333)

It was no unusual thing for a single combat to take place before a battle. Perhaps the reward for the winner was that the opposing army took the victory as an omen and were thereby discouraged. At any rate, before the English and Scottish armies fought at Halidon Hill on July 19, 1333, a certain champion of great stature, doubtless in a plaid and with tremendous bony knees, stood forth and offered single combat to any Englishman. The word 'champion' is in this sense used as a term of chivalric valour, not as the champion in a legal trial.

The Scottish champion was a man named Turnebole, who derived the name from his feat in turning a charging bull and saving the life of Robert the Bruce.

A Norfolk knight, Sir Robert de Venale, took up the challenge, and advanced against the huge Scot carrying sword and buckler. But as he did so, with sudden inspiration, he swung his sword at a black mastiff dog which accompanied Turnebole and killed it.

This seems to have so discouraged Turnebole that he was easily beaten and quickly lost his left hand and his head to Sir Robert from Norfolk. The suspicion is left that it was the black mastiff which should have had the credit for turning the bull.

Henry, Duke of Lancaster, and Otto, Son of the Duke of Brunswick (1352)

In 1352 the Duke of Lancaster discovered that the son of the Duke of Brunswick, in Germany, had plotted to take him prisoner when he was journeying " against the enemies of Christ." He announced this in public, and Otto wrote saying that the Duke was lying.

A duel followed before the French King. The two knights had to take oaths, and the English chronicler Knighton says that before Otto took the oath there was not a handsomer or more gallant-looking knight to be seen. But no sooner had he sworn than his face fell and his cheek paled and he could hold neither shield nor sword nor lance. According to Knighton, these were the awful effects of swearing a false oath. In fact, Otto was either ill or, as some chroniclers claimed, was pretending to be ill.

Whatever the reason, the French King observed the situation and stopped the duel, commanding Otto " first to depart the lists, and so go his way."

Thirty French Knights and Thirty English Knights (1355)

With this duel, which is supposed to have taken place in 1355, we are coming more to the exact spirit of the duel of chivalry. The Lord of Beaumanoir, a famous French knight, is supposed to have taken prisoner an English knight. This Englishman acted arrogantly and expressed the usual English distaste for foreigners. He spoke slightingly of the French and declared that any Englishman was worth two Frenchmen—" Ane Ingliss man worthe Franche twa."

The Englishman then expressed a wish for a fight

between English and French with equal numbers, which hardly agreed with his boast. Beaumanoir told the Englishman to go to his countrymen and select twenty-nine companions. He would do the same among his own kinsmen, and the two companies should meet in battle. This was arranged to take place at Caen, in Normandy. " By Kayne in Normandie it was."

The Englishman gathered his twenty-nine and arrived at Caen at the appointed hour. Beaumanoir and his friends were waiting, and the Frenchman had arranged that each knight should bring his lady-love or his wife to watch the fight, for he believed that this would make his men fight bravely. Edward I would have frowned on this, for he would have wanted only knights who would fight without ladies to spur them on.

The Frenchmen had horses guarded with iron and steel hoops, but the English horses were uncovered, and so the English made ready to fight on foot. Gallantly, the Frenchmen also dismounted, and the battle began with spears. One Frenchman was killed, but after long fighting the issue was still in the balance.

A French squire then left the ranks, and the Lord of Beaumanoir shouted after him that he thought better of him than to believe that he would be the first to run away. The squire answered that one had to draw back in order to jump forward.

> " The ram oft gais a-bak
> That he the maire debaits may mak."

Illustrating this very briskly, the squire mounted his horse and charged the Englishmen, who were drawn up in the shape of a harrow, as at Crécy. The squire had seen a weak spot, and the Englishmen wavered for a few minutes against this unexpected attack. The Frenchmen quickly seized their chance, and the fight soon ended, with nine Englishmen killed, twenty-one taken prisoner, and only the one French casualty.

Whether the French squire was justified in using his horse is a matter of opinion, but the chronicler rightly draws the moral that " there is no wit in despising other nations."

Sir John Annesley and his Squire, Thomas Katrington (1380)

Near the end of the reign of Edward III Sir John Annesley made a charge of treason against his squire, Thomas Katrington, who had been keeper of a castle in France. The knight said the squire had sold the castle to the French in 1375, when he had ample men and stores to defend it. He therefore challenged his squire to do battle.

The squire was imprisoned for a time, but when Edward III was on his death-bed the squire was released. The knight protested in vain against this, but early in the reign of Richard II it was decided that in a cause arising beyond the realm and across the seas, a case of transmarine treason, the duel was a lawful way to settle the matter if it were duly notified to the Constable and the Marshal of England and fought in their presence. This, in fact, was the thing to which Parliament objected—making the Court of Chivalry competent to try a case of treason. It was certainly done against the better judgment of the lawyers and the older knights of England.

However, wooden lists were made at Westminster, " as

strong as if they had been meant to last for ever," and on June 7, 1380, a huge crowd flocked to the spectacle. It far exceeded the crowd which had witnessed the coronation of the young King Richard II three years before!

The Combat. Early in the morning the young King took his seat. " As the manner is, the knight in his armour then rode up on a charger decently caparisoned, for the appellant or accuser must enter the place first to be ready for the coming of the defendant."

What the knight did for the next hour is not clear, but after that interval the squire was called with three trumpet-blasts.

" Thomas Katrington, defendant, appear to defend thy cause for which John de Anneslee, knight and appellant, hath appealed thee in public and by writ! "

At the third trumpet-blast the squire rode out, armed, on a charger well caparisoned, and with his saddle-cloths bearing the arms of Katrington.

As he neared the lists Katrington dismounted, lest in accordance with the customs of the duel the Constable of England should claim his horse, as he was entitled to do if it entered the lists when the battle was to be fought on foot. Katrington sounds as if he may have been a very careful man to worry about his horse at such a moment, or else he had every confidence in victory, and so felt certain that he would need a horse after the fight. He was a giant of a man, whereas his lord, the knight, was small, and perhaps this gave him great confidence.

But his care was useless, " for the horse, prancing near the lists, thrust its head and neck a little over the barriers, whereupon the Constable of England, Sir Thomas of Woodstock, uncle of the young King and author of the

Ordinance governing the Court of Chivalry, claimed the horse. He swore he would have its head at any rate—that is, as much of it as had come within the lists."

The horse was granted to the Constable, and it is clear that the rules of chivalry did not stop a knight keeping a careful eye on all the perquisites he could get, even if he were both rich and high-born.

The squire entered the lists on foot, and the articles of accusation and defence were read out. He tried to make some objection, but was told that if he admitted the accuracy of the accusation and refused to fight, then he would be hanged without delay. At that Katrington blurted out that he would fight that knight not only on the single plea, but in any other quarrel he cared to make.

The usual oaths were taken, including that against magic, and prayers were offered up. Then the battle began.

They fought for a long time with spears, with swords, and finally with daggers. At last the knight disarmed the squire, gripped him in a wrestler's hug, and threw him.

But as Sir John Annesley prepared to clinch the matter by falling on the squire with the full weight of his armour a strange mishap occurred. Sir John was absolutely exhausted, and the sweat so ran down his forehead under his helmet that he could not see properly. The result was that instead of falling on his opponent he missed and fell down at his side.

Katrington was equally exhausted, but he managed to raise himself off the ground and throw his body over the knight's. But as he had not dropped from a standing position, the weight of his armour did not have its full effect.

However, a great hubbub arose as the two exhausted men stretched out on the ground like helpless animals. One faction claimed that the knight was underneath and therefore beaten. The other side declared that he would soon rise and gain the victory.

The first seems the more reasonable argument, but the King ordered that Katrington should be lifted off Sir John so that he could be raised. Sir John cried to them to leave him alone, for all was well with him. But, heave as he would, he could not shake off the squire's dead weight, and eventually the officers of the duel lifted him off.

Sir John immediately appealed to the King to allow him to be put back in the same position, with the squire over him. He had noticed that Katrington was nearly dead as the result of his efforts in the long duel and the weight and the heat of his armour. The squire also was raised, but he could neither walk nor stand unaided and had been set in a chair in the lists.

When the officers saw how eager Sir John was, and how he even offered a great sum of money if they would only do as he asked, they announced that the combatants should be put back as they were, the squire above, the knight below, " in accordance with wonted custom."

Then, dramatically, the squire fell from his chair as if he were dead. He was given wine and water, but his condition improved only when he was stripped of his armour. " Which fact proved the knight the victor, and the squire the vanquished."

But Katrington's spirit was not yet crushed, and after a long time he raised his head and glared fiercely around.

Sir John, still in full armour, came up and called him a false traitor and dared him to fight again. But Katrington was beyond fighting and was carried home to die next morning, raving mad.

One chronicler said that the result " gave delight to the people and grief to traitors," and another that proof of the justice of Sir John's cause was that the squire had died. Yet, looking back after 584 years, it does seem that Katrington was unfairly treated.

Martigo de Vileños and Sir John Walsh (1384)

Another duel of the same kind was fought in London on November 30, 1384. Martigo de Vileños, a knight from Navarre, ' appealed ' Sir John Walsh, an Englishman, of treason. In fact, the real reason was a ' close combat ' of a domestic nature between the two men, but that was not allowed to sway the final outcome.

Vileños was beaten, and, despite the plea of the Queen herself, he suffered the penalty of a false accusation of treason and was himself hanged and drawn as a traitor. It was said that after the Constable and the Marshal had condemned him the King agreed to the sentence being carried out " lest such accusations should become too many in the land."

Sir Nicholas Brembre, Mayor of London (1388)

Parliament must have disliked both these cases tried before the Court of Chivalry, and no doubt that was why the King had Vileños executed—to deter too many people from making his Court of Chivalry the excuse for trying personal quarrels on the pretext of accusations of treason. But the King was soon to see a case in which the

Members of Parliament were themselves ready to fight a duel of chivalry.

This was in 1388, when, only seven years after his popularity at the time of the defeat of Wat Tyler in 1381, the young King had made himself hated by both Parliament and the City of London. This was due largely to the way he insisted on his royal rights as against the growing rights of the people—or, at least, those of the rich merchants and the knights.

In that year, 1388, the King's party was losing power fast, and in February Sir Nicholas Brembre, Mayor of London, was accused in the King's presence of treason. Everybody knew that Brembre's real ' treason ' was not against the King, but in supporting him against Parliament.

Brembre fiercely denied the charge and offered to defend himself as a knight by fighting any chosen champion. He did not have to wait long for the challenge to be taken up.

" And on a sudden, like snow, there flew from every side of the House of Commons the gloves of knights, esquires and commons, crying with one voice: ' We also will accept the duel to prove these things to thy head.' "

But Parliament as a body did not intend to give countenance to the duel of chivalry as a form of trial for political offences. The snow-white gloves were left where they fell, and Brembre was executed as a traitor, without the chance to fight. The description here of the gloves " falling like snow," incidentally, does suggest that the gloves thrown down in such challenges were white, although the chronicler may have meant that they came down as fast as snow.

Sir David de Lindsay and John, Lord Welles (1390)

In 1389 a three years' truce was arranged between England and Scotland, and a regular traffic began between the two old enemies. Traders, pilgrims on their way to Canterbury and Rome, scholars going to Oxford and Cambridge, and knights with safe conducts to fight chivalric duels became common sights.

One of the most picturesque of all duels of chivalry took place between a Scotsman and an Englishman in 1390, the Scotsman having been given a safe conduct for the purpose of fighting. The duel took place in one of the most romantic of all settings—Old London Bridge, the bridge of twenty arches that had taken thirty-three years to build and was to last, patched up, for 622 years.

It followed a banquet in Scotland where an argument arose about courage and whether the English or the Scots were the more valorous in battle. The outcome was that the English Ambassador to the Court of the Scottish King, Lord Welles, issued a challenge to fight with sharpened points to the death, a challenge that was taken up by Sir David de Lindsay.

The combat took place on May 6, 1390. The course had been prepared on the narrow bridge. As always, a barrier of planks was erected, each knight galloping down one side and thrusting at his opponent over the planks. A dais was set aside for King Richard and his Queen and as many of his courtiers as it would hold. This was doubtless placed in one of the openings between the houses, or in a space cleared by one of the frequent fires, or else houses had been taken down for the purpose and would be rebuilt after the fight. Every available window was hired by the nobility, and the rest of the

Every Available Window was hired

people crowded in as best they could or watched from boats or the banks below.

It must have been a colourful scene: the knights in their shining armour and crested helmets; the horses draped in bright cloth and gleaming harness; the heralds in their tabards and with their trumpets; the lords and the ladies in their brilliant clothes, displaying all the colours of the rainbow; the water thundering under the twenty arches of the bridge, and the sparkling river crowded with boats and barges full of eager spectators.

Then the heralds' trumpets would sound and the two knights would spur at each other, the silence of the people broken by the tremendous thunder of hooves that must have risen even above the crashing waterfall below every arch of the bridge. With a clash that must have shaken the houses, already nearly two hundred years old, the knights met. Both spears were broken, but neither knight fell.

Lord Welles swayed a little, but Sir David sat like a man of stone, so that the people cried, " You are fixed in your saddle, Sir Knight; you are tied in your saddle! "

Sir David immediately jumped from his saddle, knelt before the King and Queen, and sprang into his saddle again with a single bound. If you wish to know what this meant you have only to look at the suit of armour of the Black Prince in Canterbury Cathedral, and you will not be surprised that this was done " to the great wonder of the beholders."

A second course was run with fresh spears. Again the spears were splintered, but " without anie great hurt on either part." At the third assault, however, Lord Welles was struck from his saddle and fell heavily, being " sore hurt."

The spectators groaned, imagining that the Scotsman would now kill the Englishman with his dagger, as he was entitled to do under the rules. Sir David was off his horse in a flash, but instead of drawing his dagger he took off Welles's helmet and held him tenderly until a doctor arrived.

The Scotsman visited the English knight's bedside daily while he was ill, and he made himself so popular that King Richard asked him to stay longer in London. His permit was renewed on May 13 and 25, and it can be taken as certain that London Bridge was again crowded with cheering spectators when the Scottish knight set off for home, this time in the ship the *Seinte Marie* of Dundee. It is not often that fighting produces such good feeling, and it is nice to know that in 1406 Sir David, then the Earl of Crawford, was made " Deputy Chamberlain of Scotland, north of the Forth."

Sir William Dalzell and Sir Piers Courtenay (about 1390)

All Scotsmen were not so chivalrous on meeting Englishmen. At about the same time Sir William Dalzell, the King of Scotland's banner-bearer, had a great reputation as a tilter. Dalzell challenged Sir Piers Courtenay, England's banner-bearer, and in the fight Dalzell purposely left his helmet unstrapped. This soon worked to his advantage because in the first two charges Sir Piers' spear struck Dalzell's helmet, which, being unlaced, avoided the full shock of the blows. In the third course Dalzell knocked out two of the Englishman's front teeth.

Now, Sir Piers was handsome and proud of it. Infuriated by the loss of his two front teeth, he complained volubly of the Scot's unfairness in having his helmet unlaced. Dalzell then offered to ride six more courses provided that conditions for both men should be exactly the same, and that a forfeit of £200 should be paid if either party broke the contract. Sir Piers, " blazing with wrath over the loss of his teeth," agreed immediately.

Then the cunning Scot told the King that as he had lost an eye at the battle of Otterburn, Sir Piers must consent to lose one of his. Of course, Sir Piers refused this, and Sir William at once claimed the £200.

After some argument and fighting King Richard ordered the £200 to be given to Sir William Dalzell, saying that he had surpassed the Englishman both in deeds and wit. Probably the King was right, for it was recorded that the Englishman was " sufficiently grandiloquent and verbose " and had been jesting somewhat ponderously at the expense of the Scots. Indeed, it is easy to recognize a modern type of Englishman in this handsome knight who was so proud of his looks and so self-satisfied and so scornful of other nations.

Henry, Duke of Hereford, and Thomas, Duke of Norfolk (1398)

This duel of chivalry was a turning-point in English history. It was the point at which King Richard II's fondness for the duel of chivalry was to catch up with him. He had flouted the lawyers by allowing the Court of Chivalry to adjudge trials of treason under the duel of chivalry, and the fact had not been forgotten. This famous duel stirred up criticism against the King and helped to decide his fate.

In 1398 Henry, Duke of Hereford, appealed the Duke of Norfolk of high treason in that he had used words tending to the King's dishonour. Norfolk denied the charge. King Richard had good reason to fear Hereford's ambition, and he must have wondered what was behind a challenge that had Hereford as champion of the King's good name. The King fixed September 16, 1398, as the date for the duel.

Great preparations were made. The mail and the armour were fashioned in Milan and Nuremberg, and the lists, fenced round with a moat, were erected at Coventry. A multitude of spectators gathered in eager anticipation on the appointed day.

Hereford, the accuser, came first to the barriers fully armed, mounted on a white horse covered with blue and green velvet. He was the man the people favoured. In answer to the Constable and the Marshal, Hereford said that he had come to do his devoir against the Duke of Norfolk as a false traitor. He swore on the Gospels that his quarrel was true and just, then, sheathing his naked sword, he put down his visor, made the sign of the Cross on his forehead, and entered the lists, spear in hand.

Not long after the King took his seat on the staging. He appeared to be in joyful mood, and those nearest to him knew that this was because soothsayers had prophesied that the Duke of Norfolk would win. Ten thousand armed men were in attendance to keep order.

Norfolk was hovering " on horsebacke at the entery of the listes," his charger barbed with crimson velvet. Like Hereford, he took the oath, and as he entered the lists he said aloud, " God aide hym that hath the rights."

It seems that when he saw the two men facing each

49

other King Richard suddenly lost faith in his soothsayers. He had a feeling that the Duke of Hereford would win, and he knew that would be dangerous for himself—or else there was something in his mind that we know nothing about.

The King took the apparently strange course of stopping the duel and banishing both men. Hereford was banished for ten years, Norfolk for life. It does seem that Richard meant to keep Norfolk out of harm's way for a time and then call him back.

Whatever the King's intention, Norfolk never did return: he soon died in Venice. As for Hereford, he came back the next year with an army at his back. He was welcomed, and became King Henry IV, while Richard II, whose reign had begun in such a burst of popularity, was deposed and later foully put to death.

The Deposition of King Richard II and the Royal Champion

" In the silence of dark midnight, weeping and lamenting that he had ever been born," Richard was taken hurriedly from what had been his capital city, and soon after Henry IV was crowned with all the pomp that so delighted the heart of the man he had deposed.

In the ceremony the office of King's Champion was not tactfully forgotten, as we might have expected. Sir John Dymoke had acted as champion of Richard II, offering to do battle with any man who questioned his right to the throne. Henry had successfully questioned that right, but the son of Richard's champion, Sir Thomas Dymoke, acted as Henry's champion.

The post was disputed on both occasions by the Frevyle family, but the Dymoke family prevailed and received the Manor of Scrivelsby, in Lincolnshire, for so long as the King's Champion was chosen from the family.

In the midst of the Coronation banquet Sir Thomas Dymoke, fully armed and mounted on his charger, rode into the hall at Westminster, preceded by two other men bearing a naked sword and spear. He caused a herald to proclaim that if any man said his liege lord and King of England, Henry IV, was not of right crowned king he, as the King's Champion, was ready to prove the contrary with his body.

This is a relic of the duel of chivalry or trial by combat which survived in the ceremony of the Coronation to modern times, although the brave words of the King's Champion have never been taken up. It would certainly have caused a stir if the challenge had ever been accepted —in the time of the deposed Stuart kings, for example— and a still greater stir if the King's Champion had been defeated.

Bertrand Usana and John Bolomer (1407)

In 1406 Bertrand Usana, a citizen of Bordeaux, had spoken severely of the general wickedness of Englishmen, and John Bolomer accused him of treason, although if he were a Frenchman it is hard to see how this amounted to treason.

The duel was fought at Nottingham on August 12, 1407, before King Henry IV.

When the combatants were ready the Constable of England cried, " Laissez les aller, laissez les aller, laissez les aller et faire leur devoir." French was still the language of chivalry.

The chronicler says that John Bolomer, as a valiant and worthy knight, fell manfully upon Bertrand Usana with various kinds of weapons, and Bertrand made a strenuous and brave defence. They fought for a long time, and then the King, having regard to their reputation and their years, listened to the pleading of " our dearest cousin the King of Scotland and our own sons." The King cried, " Ho, ho, ho! " the usual sign to stop, and declared that neither man should die. Neither party had earned infamy but rather honour in the fight.

John Upton and John Downe (1430)

It is not often that a lawyer is to be found sampling his own medicine, but in 1430 John Upton, a lawyer, accused John Downe, gentleman, of treason. He claimed that Downe had imagined or plotted the King's death on his coronation day, November 6, 1429. Henry VI (1422–61) had come to the throne as a baby and had not been crowned until the seventh year of his reign.

The duel took place in London on January 24, 1430, and the sheriffs of London had been ordered to prepare the lists and barriers for the fight, to level the ground with sand, and to clear away all large stones. There was again a long fight, and again a king stopped a battle.

There is no record that he commended the valour of the two men, and it is certain that King Henry VI's heart was in his mouth at every blow, for he was a most tender-hearted man by any standards and hated fighting.

He always preferred to pardon alleged offences against his royalty, as in 1445, when Thomas Fitzgerald, Prior of the Knights of St John at Kilmainham, accused James Butler, Earl of Ormonde, of treason.

The duel was arranged for October 4, but before then Henry had given the Earl a pardon. But the Prior evidently meant to have his fun, or to display his own willingness to fight for the King. On the battle day he appeared at the appointed place fully armed, " keeping the field till high noon."

John Davy and William Catur (1447)

But even King Henry VI did not interfere with a duel that was arranged in the following year (1446). It seems odd that it should rank as a duel of chivalry, because neither man was of gentle birth, but the Court of Chivalry had become so much the usual treason court, despite the opposition of Parliament, that any accused could elect to fight under its rules.

It was fought before the Constable and the Marshal of England in Smithfield, London, and arose out of certain utterances or prophecies " made and imagined " against the King, laid to the charge of a London armourer, William Catur. Catur was accused by his own servant, John Davy, and the duel was fought on January 31, 1447.

The armourer had many well-meaning friends, and that was his undoing. These friends bought Catur so much Malmsey wine and *aqua vita* to comfort him that it was the cause of his downfall and their discomfort. For Catur " poured in so much wine that when he came into the place in Smithfield where he should fight both his wit and his strength failed him. Although he was a tall and hardy man, he was so overloaded with hot drink that he was beaten by his servant, Davy, who was only a coward and a wretch." Catur's body was drawn to Tyburn on a hurdle and there hanged and beheaded.

John Davy, the servant, did not long outlive his master. He was hanged shortly after at Tyburn for stealing, and John Stow, the historian, makes no bones about saying that he was a false servant. " Let such false accusers note this example," Stow says, " and let them look for no better end without speedie repentance. Myself have had the like servant that likewise accused me of many articles. He liveth yet, but hath hardly escaped hanging since. God make him penitent."

But the fact remains that the servant had beaten his master in the fight, and it is plain that nobody believed that God indicated the right in a duel of treason-chivalry, as they used to believe He did in a trial by combat.

Sir James Parker and Sir Hugh Vaughan (1492)

What is believed to be the last duel of chivalry fought in England took place in 1492, and it was a fitting example of how such affairs wasted good knights. It was a quarrel between Sir James Parker and Sir Hugh Vaughan about the arms the Garter King had given to Sir Hugh. Henry VII (1485–1509) was holding a great tournament at Richmond, probably against his better judgment, for, like Edward I, he was a king who hated waste and showiness.

But he allowed the duel to be fought, and in the first charge Sir James Parker was slain. His helmet broke before Vaughan's spear, " and he was so stricken into the mouth that his tongue was borne into the hinder part of his head, and so he died incontinently."

And with Sir James Parker died the duel of chivalry in England.

I

A SOCIAL ACCOMPLISHMENT

It is perhaps natural that since men had seen the duel used as an instrument of justice in courts of law for some six hundred years, they should come to use it as a final resort of appeal for their private disputes.

THE LAW FROWNS ON DUELLING

In fact, the law tried to stop the habit from its start. Queen Elizabeth's Privy Council in 1580 condemned the private duel most vigorously. Their words had little effect. It was an age when men easily became drunk with their own courage, their own magnificence, and the frothy speeches that flowed naturally from their lips. The only thing that cramped the growth of the formal private duel in those days was the hot blood of the Elizabethans themselves. Usually rapiers were out and the quarrel was settled in the street without the formality of arranging a duel. And, as Shakespeare's Mercutio says in *Romeo and Juliet*, the cause of the quarrel was often trifling:

> Thou! Why, thou wilt quarrel with a man that hath a hair more, or a hair less, in his beard than thou hast; thou wilt quarrel with a man for cracking nuts, having no other reason but because thou hast hazel eyes. . . . Thou hast quarrelled with a man for coughing in the street, because he hath wakened thy dog that hath lain asleep in the sun. Didst

thou not fall out with a tailor for wearing his new doublet before Easter? with another for tying his new shoes with old riband? . . .

That being the explosive state of gentlemen wearing swords, it is no wonder that the Privy Council decided to act. They declared that the disregard of their previous warning had brought contempt on them, so that persons were not at all afraid to appeal others to single combat upon every trifling occasion. Therefore they ordered proclamation to be made prohibiting challenges to single combat.

A Duellist Executed

Severe action was promised, and before the year was out the Scots had followed the English example. In Edinburgh a surgeon who had killed his opponent in a duel was found guilty of murder and condemned to death— " his heid to be strykkin fra his bodie."

This was confirmed in a Scots Act of November 15, 1600, " anent singular combattis." It spoke of the great liberty that " sundry persons take in provoking others to singular combats upon sudden and frivolous quarrels," and promised an ignominious death to anybody who broke the new law. This was applied without mercy to the unlucky surgeon in Edinburgh.

Executions fail to stop Duelling

But it is remarkable how ineffectual the death sentence has always been in stopping any offence. In 1722 Sir George Mackenzie said that private duels " are but illustrious and honourable murders." The law always took the view that duelling was plain murder, with nothing illustrious or honourable about it. Culprits were supposed to be prosecuted, even though the duel seemed to be the favourite pastime of Society gentlemen, and was reported in all the newspapers. Even in the Army the authorities were always very much against duelling— on paper.

(b) THE PRIVATE DUEL AND SOCIETY

In the two and a half centuries that followed 1600 duelling so flourished among the upper classes that it became a social accomplishment with its own code of rules. Indeed, it was more than a social accomplishment, it was necessary to life. If a gentleman ever refused a challenge—any challenge, no matter how trifling or malicious—then he might as well hang himself from the nearest tree. He would never again be able to hold up his head in public. The social pressure exerted by duelling can be measured by the many famous men, such as Charles James Fox and the Duke of Wellington, who were against duelling and yet were forced to answer personal challenges to fight to the death. The same state of affairs existed even more strongly in the young and democratic United States of America. It was not merely an aristocratic privilege there, but common to most classes of men.

As time passed the law was constantly thwarted by the juries. No matter how sternly the judge summed up against the duellist accused of murder, if the duel had been fought fairly the jury almost invariably refused to bring in a verdict of murder. Public opinion was in favour of ' a bit of sport,' and the jurymen probably argued that if the gentlemen had agreed to shoot each

E 2

other or stick each other with swords and provide entertainment for their inferiors, there was no reason to stop them. Duelling might be ridiculous, but they would not hang a man for being ridiculous—and, moreover, had he not risked his own life? In any case, plain men refused to class duellists with poisoners and cut-throats who worked in the dark. The law is always frustrated and defeated when it is in advance of public opinion.

The Private Duel becomes a Craze

The custom of the private duel, like so many others, came to England from France, probably during the reign of Francis I (1515–47). It was as early as 1547 that one of the most famous duels of all time was fought. This was between the Chevaliers de Jarnac and de la Châtaigneraye, two favourite courtiers of the King, and Jarnac won by means of a ' sly ' cut. Their armour reached only to the knee, and by letting his sword slip Jarnac ' hamstrung '— that is, cut both calves of—his opponent and left him helpless. This ' cut of Jarnac ' was argued about for years.

Francis I approved of duelling, and is said to have challenged the Emperor Charles V.

It is believed that during the reign of Henry IV (1589–1610) four thousand gentlemen were killed in duels and fourteen thousand pardons were issued for breaking the law against duelling!

Yet severe examples were made. Praslin, son of a distinguished officer of state, was banished, and Francis de Montmorenci, Count of Boutteville, a crazy duellist, was executed on a public scaffold because he defied the law about duelling, but it need hardly be said that this had little permanent effect on its popularity.

The figures above certainly justify Alexandre Dumas, whose musketeers made duelling as necessary to life as breathing, and another French writer, Montaigne. Montaigne said that " if three Frenchmen were placed in the Libyan desert they would not be a month there without quarrelling and fighting."

Hardly a day passed in Paris without several deaths by duelling, and an English ambassador, Lord Herbert of Cherbury, himself a lively duellist, said that " during his long residence in France, he hardly met a Frenchman who had not killed his man in a duel."

The fashion reached its height during the reigns of Louis XIII (1610–43) and Louis XIV, the Sun King (1643–1715). It was said that the usual greeting was not " What is the news? " but " Do you know who fought yesterday? "

The Craze reaches England. The climax of the duel in England came rather later, although duelling arrived with the accession of James I (1603–25). The King frowned on duelling officially, and yet he could speak of " bewitching duels." It received a check in the time of Cromwell, whose son-in-law, Ireton, is said to have allowed his nose to be pulled in public and refused to fight. With the Restoration of Charles II in 1660, however, duelling became a fashionable craze in England.

Duelling becomes a Public Spectacle

Ballrooms, masquerades, theatres, the open streets, and the many fields in the towns—duels were staged there every day. Covent Garden, Chalk Farm, Lincoln's Inn Fields, and Hampstead Heath became the favourite spots in London for the actual fight, and a club was formed to which nobody was admitted who had not killed his man in a duel, and so proved himself a 'man of honour.'

The practice spread to all kinds of gentlemen, and, as some modern doctors smoke, so doctors of those days duelled with swords or pistols, although, through having attended at so many duels, they knew the dangers better than most men.

Code of Conduct

Duels were sometimes vicious or ill-tempered or even fraudulent, but it is remarkable how often the duellists displayed courage, great fortitude, politeness, and even kindness to the men whose blood they had spilled or were trying to spill.

Some of the accounts are touching, and the reader is uncertain whether to shed tears at the sight of men persisting to the death in a course society told them was honourable, but which they inwardly suspected to be criminal and foolish, or to tear his hair in despair at their foolishness and lack of moral independence.

An odd one here and there did adopt a course of passive resistance—that is, he objected to the duelling, and declared that although he could not resist the social pressure that made him accept the challenge, he would not fire. Such a duellist, the bravest of all and the most truly 'honourable,' went out, accepted his opponent's fire, and refused to fire his own pistol. Even among the savage duellists of America there were some who made this gesture of dissent.

And, of course, although the English are sometimes accused of being heavy and humourless, humour will always break through in whatever they do, no matter how pig-headed and foolish it may be.

Two doctors, Mead and Woodward, fought a duel with swords in Gresham College. Woodward slipped and fell.

" Take your life," Dr Mead said, generously drawing back.

" Anything but your medicine," replied the fallen and ungrateful Dr Woodward.

If this story is not true, then it certainly ought to be.

Climax of the Duel of Honour

But the real heyday of the duel arrived with the first Hanoverian king, who came to this country in 1714. Political and religious spite often made the fighting vicious, even over the most trivial matters. It is reckoned that in the reign of George III (1760–1820) 172 duels were recorded, in which 69 men were killed and 96 wounded, 46 of them desperately. Note that this refers only to recorded duels—there must have been many more.

A young gentleman was not properly educated unless he had qualified with the pistols. It was much more necessary for him to do so than to take a college degree. Two questions were always asked about an unknown young man in Society: " What is his family? Has he ever blazed? "

Such social qualifications are not accepted without the consent of women. Duelling, like war, was a problem that women might have been expected to help solve, but in fact they appear to have done nothing. They helped rather to increase the evil by foolishly flocking round any man who had shown himself a ' man of honour ' by killing his opponent in a duel, as they have always flocked round a military uniform. Lysistrata did at least set herself and the Athenian women against war, but there is no record that any woman ever opposed duelling, not even when her husband had been uselessly slaughtered and she was left with small children to bring up on her own. As will be seen, even the pioneer women of the United States accepted the ' code of honour ' as a law of nature.

It is hard for us to understand the power of this social code which insisted that a man must answer any challenge, even if he could not handle a pistol or a sword and knew that his opponent was a crack shot or swordsman who had provoked the quarrel for the express purpose of taking his life.

It is only necessary to read the accounts that follow in this book to realize how strong this social law must have been. Indeed, it rather increased as time went on, when the duel began to lose favour, and the case that best drives home the strength of the custom is probably that of Ensign Sarsfield in India. This occurred as recently as 1842, when Queen Victoria had been on the throne for five years.

In these modern times, which seem to us so much better than the past, we are inclined to assume that all possible progress has been made. The same assumption was doubtless made by the Elizabethans and even the Normans, nine hundred years ago. But the comparatively recent case of Ensign Sarsfield should make us wonder how many equally solemn and foolish customs we still accept without question which future generations will regard with horror or bewildered amusement.

2

SOME HISTORIC DUELS OF HONOUR

(a) In the Days of the Stuarts (1603–1714)

Many duels were known to have been fought in this period, but unfortunately few records were kept and the details given are usually mere 'blood-and-thunder' details of how many wounds each man received and where the blood ran.

Both Duellists killed

In 1609 two of King James I's favourites met at Canonbury, which was then a country district outside the walls of London. Later, when built up, it became a fashionable area, then deteriorated into a slum, and is now once again becoming fashionable.

The two young men were Sir George Wharton and Sir James Stewart, who was a godson of the King. Details are unknown, but the result was even more wasteful than usual. The fight was so desperate that both men were killed. King James was much grieved and ordered them both to be buried in one grave, the burial being recorded in the Islington Parish Registers: " Sir George Wharton, sonne of Lord Wharton, was buried the 10th of November, 1609; James Stewart, Esq., god-sonne to King James, was buried the 10th November, 1609."

Englishmen Abroad

In the same year Sir Hatton Cheek, second in command of the English army at the siege of Juliers, quarrelled with Sir Thomas Dutton, an officer of inferior rank. They met on the sands at Calais, and Cheek insisted on fighting. They stripped to their shirts and fought with rapier and dagger so fiercely that Dutton was badly wounded and Cheek was killed.

There was another bloodthirsty affair between the future Earl of Dorset and Lord Kinloss in 1613, in which Kinloss was killed, and another in 1662, between Mr Jermyn and Colonel Howard. This was fought in the old Pall Mall, St James's, London, and was against the rules in that Mr Jermyn, the challenged party, was never told how he had offended. This was evidently an extreme case of the attitude " Never mind the ball, let's get on with the game! " It is satisfactory to know that Mr Jermyn was only severely wounded, although his second, Colonel Giles Rawlings, who must have been doubly in the dark, was killed. In the early days it was the custom for seconds as well as principals to fight.

Sir Henry Bellasis and Mr Tom Porter (1667)

In 1667 Sir Henry Bellasis fought a Mr Tom Porter after both had been drinking heavily. These two men were the greatest friends in the world, but that did not stop them fighting in Covent Garden over nothing and presenting the most touching spectacle of friendship imaginable. Tom Porter was wounded, and then he gave Sir Henry his death-wound.

Sir Henry gallantly called his opponent and kissed him and bade him make his escape. " Tom, thou hast killed me," says he, " but I will make shift to stand on my legs till thou mayest withdraw and the world not take notice of thee. I would not have thee troubled for what thou hast done."

Sir Henry Bellasis duly died, and Samuel Pepys said of the event, " It is pretty to see how the world talks of them as a couple of fools, that killed one another out of love."

The King's Dwarf

But probably the most interesting duel recorded in this period was that between Jeffery Hudson, King Charles I's dwarf, and a Mr Crofts. Queen Henrietta Maria had begged Hudson from the Duke of Buckingham when the little man had stepped out of a pie prepared for the entertainment of the King and Queen. Hudson became an important man at Court and a little too big for his boots, small as they were. But he must have been a pugnacious little bantam, for in the Civil War the King appointed him to the command of a troop of horse. When Queen Henrietta fled to France, Hudson was sent with her, and it was there that he fought Mr Crofts.

A comic poem had been written describing a fight between Hudson and a turkey-cock in which Hudson was supposed to have saved himself only by running. Mr Crofts, a young officer attached to the Queen's suite, chaffed the dwarf about the turkey-cock, and this led to high words, Hudson being very touchy about his dignity. The dwarf challenged Crofts to fight a duel, and the meeting was fixed for the following morning. Crofts brought a water-squirt as his weapon, no doubt intending to pass the affair off as a joke, but the dwarf was so enraged that he insisted on fighting Crofts with pistols on horseback.

Now, this put Crofts at a grave disadvantage, as he was a big man and it would be much easier for the dwarf to hit him than for the dwarf to be hit. It is said that Lord Erskine, a very little man, once issued a challenge to a tall and stout officer, which the latter declined on the ground that the advantage would be all with Lord Erskine. Erskine proposed at once that the size of his body should be chalked out on his opponent's body, and that all shots outside that mark should not count!

The officer was not so simple as to accept, and it is a pity that Mr Crofts was not so careful. Jeffery Hudson killed his opponent with the first bullet, which went straight through Crofts' heart. Sir Walter Scott, in one of his novels, made the dwarf full of remorse, and it is certainly true that from that moment Hudson never prospered.

(*b*) In the Days of the Hanoverians (1714–1837)

In this period, especially during its last fifty years, we have come to the palmy days of the duel in England, and, with the coming of news-sheets, much read in the fashionable coffee-houses, the records are fairly full. The difficulty is that duels were so common that the newspapers did not always give them much space, even when the rank of the contestants was high. When the Dukes of Bedford and Buckingham fought at the Gravel Pits, Kensington, the duel was given a little more news space because the two noblemen were alarmed by a notice which said, " Rubbish shot here." But this joke certainly sounds like a remark inserted by a reporter to fill space. Often newspapers allowed only six lines to describe how two gentlemen met, quarrelled, fought, and whether " one was taken, and the other left," or which one took the coffee in the ' pistols-for-two-coffee-for-one ' arrange ment.

The ' Age of Reason '

It is curious that it was unfashionable in the eighteenth century to be ' enthusiastic ' or ' passionate ' about anything. A classic calm was cultivated, and there are good grounds for calling it the Age of Reason (and also the Age of Dirt). The fact is, of course, that no period of the past is ever the ' Age ' of any one thing. All sorts of things exist cheek by jowl, some of which may be forward-looking and some relics of centuries far back.

Certainly ' classic calm ' is the last thing that would occur to anybody reading the accounts of these duels. Englishmen in those days seemed to be as passionate as any Latin race. Swords were drawn on the slightest excuse, and often two men quarrelling would be joined by twenty.

Outside the Royal Chocolate House in St James's Street, London, in 1717, during a general ' free-for-all,' three gentlemen were killed and Colonel Cunningham was saved from death only by his footman, who rushed through the drawn swords and carried his master off bodily, probably receiving a ' dressing-down ' for interfering. In 1720 one hundred gentlemen fought with swords and canes, and the Life Guards were called out

The Lukewarm, Timid Duel

From a contemporary engraving by Cruikshank

(*Mansell Collection*)

and had to kill several of the raging gentlemen before order could be restored. The row had started over two chairmen—the carriers of sedan chairs—which was just as if two gentlemen nowadays had hailed the same taxi. A week later four young bucks stopped a sedan chair and tried to kidnap a lady. A watchman who tried to help her was stabbed to death.

It is the lukewarm, timid duel that is most rarely met, the duel described by the lampoonist when he wrote:

> Great Chatham with his sabre drawn
> Stood waiting for Sir Richard Strachan;
> Sir Richard, longing to be at 'em,
> Stood waiting for the Earl of Chatham.

This does seem a most peculiar Age of Reason, but the fact is that the tag 'Age of Reason' came from the intellectual habits of the day. The social fashions were a world apart, and duelling was very much a social fashion. That a social fashion sometimes has a terrible power of life and death can easily be seen by even the most casual glance at the accounts of private duels which follow. It should be understood that these duels are a selection made by the author. They represent only a fraction of the duels fought and recorded in this period.

Dr Young and an Army Officer from the Woolwich Garrison (1720)

This is one of the earliest duels recorded in the period, and it is perhaps as well to start with a humorous episode. Most of the humour we shall come across later is tragi-comic.

Vauxhall, a little way up the river Thames from the Houses of Parliament, is grimy and squalid now, but in 1720 it was famous for its gardens. The fashionable men and women of the time sauntered along its leafy paths at most hours of the day and night, or danced cotillions or minuets or Sir Roger de Coverleys to lively orchestras. Anybody with pretensions in the social world had to go to Vauxhall.

A Dr Young was taking some ladies to Vauxhall by water, and to entertain them he played his flute. Behind them came some officers in another boat, and as they drew near the doctor happened to stop playing. One of the officers asked why the deuce he had stopped playing.

" For the same reason I started—to please myself," Dr Young answered, not unreasonably.

The officer took this very badly, and told Dr Young to keep on playing or else he would throw him in the water. To keep the peace Dr Young played all the way to Vauxhall, where both parties landed and went their different ways.

Later the doctor saw the officer walking alone, and at once went up to him and challenged him to a duel the next morning with swords.

" To prove that courage may be found under a black coat as well as a red coat, we will meet without seconds," the doctor said. " Then we can be certain that nobody will interfere with us, and we can fight to the death."

To fight without seconds was against the recognized rules of duelling, but the officer agreed, and the two men met the next morning as arranged. The officer took his ground and drew his sword, doubtless with a frightening scowl, and then was appalled to see that the doctor had pulled out a horse-pistol and was pointing it at his head.

" What, sir, do you mean to assassinate me? " the officer cried.

" No, not unless you force me to it. But you shall put up your sword and dance me a minuet, otherwise you are a dead man," the doctor answered.

The officer swore he would do no such thing, but the doctor gave him until he had counted thirty. Before he had reached ten the sword was back in its sheath, and before twenty the officer was gravely dancing a stately minuet to a tune solemnly whistled by the doctor. At least, the minuet was as stately as could be expected from a man dancing alone and with a loaded horse-pistol a few feet from his head.

After a quarter of an hour the doctor told the officer they were quits. " You forced me to play against my will; I compelled you to dance against yours. Now I will give you any other satisfaction. The next affair, of course, must be with seconds. You know where to find me. Good morning to you."

But the doctor heard no more. The officer had evidently decided, with much wisdom, that the least said the better.

Major Oneby and Mr Gower (1720)

But duels and fights, not conducted with the humour of Dr Young, were becoming so frequent that the authorities determined to make an example of somebody. The next offender who happened to present himself was a Major Oneby.

In the year 1720 Major Oneby was sitting in a London tavern playing at hazard with four other men, one of whom was a Mr Gower and another a Mr Rich. Rich offered to bet three half-crowns, at which Gower jokingly laid down three halfpence. Major Oneby then betted against Rich with three half-crowns and lost them.

Red with rage, the Major turned to Gower and said, " It was an impertinent thing to set down halfpence, and you are an impertinent puppy! "

" Whoever says so is a rascal! " Gower answered.

" You are an impertinent puppy ! "

On this, the gallant Major took up a bottle and threw it at Gower's head, but only knocked some of the powder off his wig. Gower replied by throwing a candlestick, which also missed, and both men went for their swords, which hung up in the room.

The other men stopped the Major from drawing, and

Gower then threw aside his sword. They all sat down again and played for another hour, after which Gower said to Major Oneby, " We have had hot words and you were the aggressor, but I think we may pass it over."

But the Major ungraciously answered, " No, confound you, I will have your blood."

After the reckoning was paid all the company left except Major Oneby, who called out to Gower as he was leaving, " Young man, I have something to say to you."

Gower returned, the door was shut against the others, who heard a clash of swords, and it was then that the Major gave Gower his death-wound.

On his death-bed Gower was asked if he had received his wounds in a fair fight. Apparently with some vague idea that it would be sporting to exonerate the Major, and yet not quite seeing his way because the Major was so obviously the one at fault, the dying man answered, " I think I did."

Upon these facts Major Oneby was tried and found guilty of wilful murder, " he having acted upon malice and deliberation, and not from sudden passion." He was sentenced to death, but cheated the hangman by committing suicide.

It is a fact that only three British duellists have been sentenced to death in modern times. In the case of Major Campbell, one of the others, in 1808, and in the above instance the duel was fought in a room without witnesses or seconds.

Lord Hervey and Lord Cobham (1750)

This was not a duel, but a challenge followed by an apology, and was related by Horace Walpole in 1750.

73   F 2

Walpole wrote:

About ten days ago, at the new Lady Cobham's assembly, Lord Hervey was leaning over a chair talking to some woman and holding his hat in his hand. Lord Cobham came up and spit in it—yes, spit in it—and then, with a loud laugh, turned to Nugent and said: " Pay me my wager." In short, he had laid a guinea that he would commit this absurd brutality, and that it would not be resented. Lord Hervey, with good temper and sense, asked if he had any further occasion for his hat. " Oh, I see you are angry," Cobham said. " Not very well pleased," Hervey answered.

Hervey was a young man of considerable wit and ability, but not in good health. He lived on milk and biscuits, and in those hard-drinking days it is not surprising that he was considered effeminate. No doubt Cobham had been relying on this, and he was evidently shocked when Hervey challenged him to a duel. He made abject apologies, both verbal and written, it being not quite such an offence then to refuse a challenge as it became later in the century.

Perhaps the most interesting fact in the whole affair is that the Lord Cobham who acted so disgracefully was a gentleman of ' standing ' in his party, and had been made a Field-Marshal in 1742. We have Field-Marshals who act somewhat eccentrically, but it is impossible to imagine such conduct from any present-day holder of the baton. It is poetic justice that, for all his later honours, Lord Cobham was ever after generally known as *Lord Gob'em*.

John Wilkes, M.P., and Mr Samuel Martin (1763)

It is always interesting to meet a man vaguely remembered from school history books, but in a very different situation. Most of us will know John Wilkes as the editor of that outspoken journal the *North Briton*, and as an argumentative, ' sea-lawyer ' sort of man, very ready to speak up for rights and liberties. You do not expect to meet such a man with a bullet in his stomach: that kind usually confines himself to words.

Not so John Wilkes, and when, in November 1763, he considered that he had been insulted by Samuel Martin, late Secretary to the Treasury, in the House of Commons, he sent a fierce letter, signed " your humble servant."

By return, on the very same day, John Wilkes received a satisfactory letter from Samuel Martin, calling him a malignant and infamous scoundrel. Mr Martin suggested an immediate meeting in Hyde Park with a brace of pistols each. In fact, Mr Martin was so eager that he delivered the answer himself, and said he would go straight on to the Ring in Hyde Park, where he would await Mr Wilkes and his brace of pistols, but he did not forget to sign the letter " your humble servant."

When the gentlemen had met in Hyde Park they walked together a little, concealing their pistols, to avoid some friends who seemed anxious for their company. When they were alone Mr Martin fired first and missed, while Mr Wilkes's pistol only flashed in the pan. Each took another pistol. Mr Wilkes missed, apparently having a better aim with his tongue or his pen than his pistol, but the ball from Mr Martin's pistol lodged in Mr Wilkes's belly, and he bled freely.

Mr Martin hurried up and wanted to help all he could. Mr Wilkes replied that Mr Martin had behaved like a man of honour, that he, Wilkes, was a dead man, and that

Mr Martin was to make his immediate escape. He could rest assured that nobody should know from him how the wound had been inflicted. Mr Martin took the advice, and Mr Wilkes was carried home. He scrupulously kept his promise, merely saying that he had his wound in an " affair of honour."

Mr Martin fled to Paris, the House of Commons expressed official concern at the fate of Mr Wilkes, probably somewhat to his surprise, and that august body announced itself as officially gratified when Mr Wilkes recovered. Indeed, there was a further comforting sequel in that, when Mr Wilkes next visited Paris, notes and a friendly visit were exchanged between the two men.

Lord Kilmaurs and a French Officer (1765)

This duel took place in Marseilles. Lord Kilmaurs, eldest son of the Earl of Glencairn, was renowned for his good nature, but he was deaf. At the theatre one evening he talked rather loudly to the person he was with, as deaf people often do. This offended a French officer in the same box, who gave the usual " Pray be quiet " to his lordship. The Englishman, however, carried on blissfully, not hearing a word. The officer then shouted, " Taisez-vous! " or " Hold your tongue! " which is rough talk in any language.

His lordship did hear this, and said to the Frenchman, " You have no right to order silence. I shall show my contempt for your insolence by talking still louder."

Like the blue-blooded Briton he was, his lordship proceeded to do just this, which could not have been much appreciated by the other people who had paid to listen to the play.

The French officer then left the box, and soon Lord Kilmaurs entered another box, it being the custom to move from one box to another for social chit-chat. His lordship happened to enter the same box as the French officer, and, looking about him as he entered, cast his eyes directly on the officer.

Now, Lord Kilmaurs must have been an extreme example of the absent-minded, aloof Englishman, for he failed to recognize the Frenchman. It can also be assumed that he had the sort of supercilious air about him that goes with a monocle, and it is not surprising that the French officer took his lordship's glance as impudent and provoking.

He therefore went up to the English lord and said in French, " What do you mean by staring at me? " Lord Kilmaurs, who must have thought all the world was against him that night, answered, " I think I can look at anybody."

The French officer promptly flew into a rage, saying that he would not be so treated, and dragged Lord Kilmaurs out of the box and the theatre into the street. There the Frenchman challenged him to a duel and drew his sword. His lordship was not so deaf that he could not hear that challenge to his honour, and his sword was out in a flash.

It was a colourful scene, for the theatre was in an open square near the Canebière, with the lights from the cafés shining on the gay clothes of the customers at the tables outside, the coloured window-awnings fluttering in the breeze, and the waters of the Mediterranean rolling up the shore a few yards away.

But poor Lord Kilmaurs did not have a chance to

appreciate the picturesqueness of the setting, for, after a very few passes had been exchanged, he was run through the body, the Frenchman's sword coming out at his shoulder-blade.

Immediately all was confusion. A shrieking crowd gathered, and the guard rushed up under the Marquis de Pacquigny. The Englishman was gasping for air, and the stupid crowd, as crowds always do, pressed still closer. But the Marquis ordered his men to make a ring round his English *vis-à-vis*, and so saved the English lord's life, although it looked all up with him at the time. A doctor who was in the theatre slit open the collar of Lord Kilmaurs' shirt and had him lifted up, but nobody thought he would live.

However, such is the resilience of Englishmen of the type of Lord Kilmaurs that within three days he was out of danger and the French officer was prudently out of the country.

The British Ambassador at Paris was given power to manage the matter as he thought proper, and His Excellency allowed it to drop as quietly as possible, doubtless at the request of Lord Kilmaurs. There is something ridiculous in having a sword run through your body because you happen to be deaf and because your stare is unintentionally haughty.

William, Fifth Lord Byron, and Mr Chaworth (1765)

As in the case of John Wilkes and Mr Martin, it was quite common early on in the heyday of the duel for one to be fought without seconds, and this duel was another of this kind. It was obviously desirable that there should be seconds to act as witnesses and secure fair play, and

78

it later became the custom to have seconds to arrange the time and the place of meeting and the other necessary details.

Lord Byron and Mr Chaworth, a rich country squire, were neighbours in Nottinghamshire, and it was their custom to meet other neighbours at the Star and Garter tavern in Pall Mall, at what was called the Nottinghamshire Club.

On January 26, 1765, the usual gathering was in progress, attended by ten gentlemen of unimpeachable credentials, all notables of the county.

They dined at four o'clock, as usual, and the rule of the club was to have a bill and a bottle brought in at seven. Up to that hour all was jollity and good humour, but then the question of the best way to preserve game came up for discussion.

Everybody spoke coolly except Mr Chaworth and Lord Byron, who became more and more heated. Chaworth was all for severity against poachers, while Lord Byron said the best way to care for game was to take no care of it—a principle far in advance of the times. Chaworth insisted that Sir Charles Sedley and himself had more game on five acres than Lord Byron had on all his manors.

Lord Byron offered to bet Chaworth one hundred guineas, and Chaworth insultingly called for pens, ink, and paper to put the bet into writing. After an awkward silence another gentleman pointed out that the bet could hardly be decided. Who was going round to count the pheasants, hares, partridges, and what-not on the estates?

Lord Byron was naturally and obviously irritated at Chaworth's wanting to put the bet into writing, as if he could not trust the noble lord's honour, and Chaworth rubbed salt into the wound by carrying on the argument. He declared that were it not for Sir Charles Sedley's care and his own, Lord Byron would not have a hare on his estate. Lord Byron managed a sarcastic smile, and asked what Sir Charles Sedley's manors were? Chaworth included Bulwell in the list he gave, a manor claimed by Lord Byron.

Then Chaworth said heatedly, " If you want information with respect to Sir Charles Sedley's manors he lives at Mr Cooper's in Dean Street, and I doubt not will be ready to give you satisfaction. As to myself, your lordship knows where to find me in Berkeley-row."

There was another stupefied pause, and each gentleman hurriedly fell into chat with his neighbour, but the argument stopped. Chaworth called to settle the reckoning, as was his custom, but in marking the book he was apparently so flustered that he made the mistake of marking Lord Byron absent, which would have meant his lordship's paying a fine of five shillings. The mistake was pointed out by another member, and Chaworth altered the entry, but it must have seemed to Lord Byron that it had been done purposely.

The company dispersed, and as Chaworth went out he asked another member if he thought he had been short in talking to Lord Byron. The member answered that he had gone rather too far upon so trifling a subject, but he did not believe that Lord Byron or the company would think any more about it.

Chaworth turned to go down the stairs, and Lord Byron, coming out almost immediately, met him on the stairs. It is doubtful which gentleman made the challenge, but both went to the first landing, and both called the waiter to show them to an empty room. The waiter opened the door himself, and, placing a small tallow candle on the table, then withdrew, at which the two gentlemen entered and closed the door after them.

Within a few minutes the bell rang, the waiter ran up, and, seeing the dreadful catastrophe that had occurred, hurried for his master. The two gentlemen were found standing with drawn swords, clasping each other with the other hand. A surgeon was hastily sent for, but Chaworth said that he had not many hours to live.

He further declared that he forgave Lord Byron and hoped that the world would also forgive him. He said that the affair had passed almost in the dark, only a tallow candle burning in the room. Lord Byron had asked if he meant the conversation on the game to be referred to Sir Charles Sedley or to him? Chaworth said he answered that if anything was to be said the door had better be shut. While he was doing this Lord Byron told him to draw, and, turning from the door, Chaworth saw his lordship's sword half drawn. At that, Chaworth said, he whipped out his own sword and made the first pass. The sword went through his lordship's waistcoat, and Chaworth thought he had killed Lord Byron, but as he was asking if his lordship was dangerously hurt Lord Byron shortened his sword and stabbed him in the belly.

Chaworth later lamented his own folly in fighting in the dark. He was much the better swordsman, but he thus gave up his advantage, and that was how he came to make the mistake of believing he had stabbed his lordship in the breast when he was " only entangled in his waistcoat."

On the next morning, a Sunday, Chaworth made his will and died.

Lord Byron was tried by his peers, and behaved with perfect propriety. He would not besmirch Mr Chaworth's behaviour any more than was absolutely necessary for his defence, and, expressing his deep and unfeigned sorrow, surrendered himself with the utmost confidence to the justice and humanity of their lordships.

The confidence was justified, for the peers found Lord Byron guilty of manslaughter only, which meant that, under a statute of Edward VI, he was immediately dismissed on paying his fees.

This Lord Byron was the great-uncle of the famous poet, and it was the death of this lord's son in Corsica in 1794 that brought the title to the poet. Another interesting sequel is that the poet proposed marriage to Mary Anne Chaworth, heiress of Annesley Hall, Nottinghamshire, in 1803. He wrote many verses to her, and pointed out that their union would heal " feuds in which blood was shed by our relatives." But it is recorded that Miss Chaworth remained unimpressed and regarded Lord Byron " as only a schoolboy," which, indeed, he was, being fifteen years of age and at Harrow in that year.

Yet the abiding impression must be of the duellists themselves, a lasting wonder that two of the most polished gentlemen in the land should behave like savages over such a trifling argument, and speak like civilized beings only after one had received his death-wound.

George Garrick and Robert Baddeley (1770)

This Garrick was brother to the famous David Garrick

" Spare him ! Oh, spare him ! "

and both duellists were actors at Drury Lane Theatre. It will be noticed that even the title ' Mr ' has been omitted from the heading. This is in accordance with the practice of those days, when all actors were strictly professionals, and not gentlemen.

Duels were not common among actors, because, it was said, they were normally so rude to each other that it would have been a lifelong occupation to avenge insults! But Baddeley accused Garrick of being too friendly with Mrs Baddeley, and the parties met in Hyde Park.

Baddeley fired his pistol first, without effect. This is not surprising as his arm is said to have been shaking like a leaf. Taking pity on his colleague, or perhaps suffering from fright himself, Garrick fired into the air (or ' deloped,' as it was called when done deliberately).

At that moment Mrs Baddeley arrived in a hackney-coach and threw herself between the combatants in a dramatic attitude, crying, " Spare him! Oh, spare him! "

The parties were so pleased with the tableau they had presented that they embraced all round and departed the greatest of friends. But the whole set-up certainly bears a sinister resemblance to modern publicity stunts worked by certain film-stars.

Richard Brinsley Sheridan, Esq., and Major Mathews (1772)

Sheridan was in love with a Miss Linley, daughter of a well-known composer, but her parents did not favour the future playwright. However, Sheridan persisted in paying court to her, and when a paragraph appeared in a Bath newspaper reflecting on her character he hastened to discover the name of the man who had inserted it.

This turned out to be a Major Mathews, well known in

fashionable circles in Bath, and a man who also had his eye on Miss Linley. Major Mathews had gone to London. Sheridan pursued him, and they fought a duel, with swords, in Henrietta Street, Covent Garden, in 1772. Courage and skill were displayed by both men, but Sheridan disarmed his opponent and forced him to sign a formal retraction of the published paragraph.

Sheridan returned to Bath, and as the insult had been publicly given he thought the apology should also be public, and he caused it to be printed in the same newspaper.

This offended Major Mathews, who returned to Bath and challenged Sheridan again. Sheridan would have been justified in declining, but he agreed, and the duel was fought on Kingsdown. They fired pistols and then fought with swords. The contest was desperate and ill-tempered. Both men were wounded, and, closing with each other, they fell to the ground, where the fight continued until they were separated. Each received several wounds, and a part of his opponent's sword was left in Sheridan's ear.

The actual result of the duel is not recorded, but Miss Linley was not proof against such double-duelled devotion, and in 1772 she ran away with Sheridan to the Continent, where they were married. It is also satisfactory to know that the ceremony was again performed after their return to England, with the consent of the lady's parents. Two years later Sheridan's great comedy *The Rivals* was produced.

The only jarring note comes from Mathews, who later claimed that the duel was a hoax, that Sheridan arrived drunk, and that he (Mathews) could have killed him with the greatest ease. The evidence seems to show that Mathews was merely a bad loser.

Count Ricé and Viscount Du Barry (1778)

In 1778 a Count Ricé was visiting the house of the Viscount Du Barry at Bath when an argument arose. The Viscount contradicted a statement of Count Ricé's by saying, " *Cela n'est pas vrai!* "

An apology was refused, and the two men immediately asked for seconds to accompany them to Claverton Down, with a surgeon. There the company remained until daylight, presumably glaring at each other's shadows in the darkness, but the cold night air did not cool them off. At dawn the ground was marked out by the seconds, and the two men faced each other, armed with two pistols and a sword each.

Viscount Du Barry fired first, and put a ball in Count Ricé's thigh. Count Ricé fired and hit the Viscount in the breast. At that the seconds might have tried to stop the affair by asking if honour was satisfied, but nothing was done. The Viscount went back two or three paces and then made for his opponent again. Both fired once more, without effect, and then drew their swords.

But before they could engage, Count Ricé saw the Viscount fall and heard him cry, " I ask for life." The Count answered, " I give it you." In a few seconds the Viscount fell back and died. Count Ricé was carried to Bath dangerously wounded, but recovered.

The Hon. Charles James Fox and Mr Adam (1779)

Charles James Fox, the famous politician, had ideas far in advance of his time, especially about tolerance and freedom, but he could not ignore a challenge, even if he did not take duelling seriously.

Fox, although he had the fashionable vices of his time, such as heavy drinking and gambling, was a man of high standards in his political conduct. A Mr Adam asked him to insert a piece in the Press to explain that remarks Fox had made in the House of Commons did not reflect personally on Adam. Fox had not intended any reflection on Adam, and it would have been the easiest thing in the world to do as he asked. But Fox refused. He said it was inconsistent with his ideas of proper conduct to explain a speech which, in his opinion, required no explanation.

Adam therefore sent his second, Major Humberstone, to arrange details of a duel, and the parties met in Hyde Park next day at 8 A.M., fighting with pistols at a distance of fourteen paces.

Fox was a tubby man, and his second said to him, "Fox, you must stand sideways to present less of a target."

"Why, man, I'm as thick one way as the other!" Fox answered.

Adam called upon Fox to fire first, but Fox answered, "I'm hanged if I do any such thing. I have no quarrel."

Adam then fired and wounded Fox in the chest, which nobody seemed to notice, except poor Fox. But the seconds asked Adam if he was satisfied, and he said, "Will Mr Fox declare he meant no personal attack on my character?" Upon which Fox said, "This is no place for apology; I desire him to go on."

Adam fired his remaining pistol, but missed. Fox fired his in the air, and then said that as the affair was ended he could say that he meant no more personal affront to

Mr Adam than he did to either of the other gentlemen then present.

Adam replied, " You have behaved like a man of honour."

Fox then mentioned that he believed himself wounded, and when his waistcoat was opened this was found to be the case, but he made light of it. It was general knowledge at the time that the ammunition supplied to the Army was poor, and Fox exclaimed, " Egad, Adam, it would have been all over with me if your pistols had not been charged with Government powder! "

The Earl of Shelburne and Colonel Fullarton (1780)

This duel is an excellent example of the way civilized men put a gloss on a barbarous custom and observed it according to such rules and strict etiquette that they made it look light and dainty, like a minuet of the period.

The only rough note was struck at the start by Colonel Fullarton, Member of Parliament for Plympton, who complained to the House of Commons of the ungentlemanly behaviour of the Earl of Shelburne. Fullarton declared that the noble Earl, " with all the aristocratic insolence that marks that nobleman's character, has dared to say that I and my regiment are as ready to act against the liberties of England as against her enemies."

There could be only one outcome of such a public remark. Two days later, at 5.30 A.M. on March 22, 1780, the parties met in Hyde Park, Lord Shelburne having Lord Frederick Cavendish for his second and Colonel Fullarton being attended by Lord Balcarres.

The first item of interest is that the two men who were to try to butcher each other walked politely together while their seconds arranged details. It is a pity that we do not know what they talked about.

Pistols were chosen and loaded carefully. Twelve paces had been agreed as the proper distance, and the two principals had to interrupt their polite walk to take up position.

Colonel Fullarton, the insulted individual, who should have fired first, politely desired Lord Shelburne to fire, which his lordship as politely declined. The seconds ordered Fullarton to fire. He did so and missed. Lord Shelburne returned the fire, also missing. The Colonel then fired his second pistol and hit his lordship in the groin, which his lordship indicated.

The seconds ran up, and Lord Cavendish offered to take the pistol from Lord Shelburne, but his lordship refused to hand over, saying, " I have not fired that pistol."

Thereupon Colonel Fullarton went back to his ground, having left it to help Lord Shelburne, and repeatedly asked his lordship to fire at him. But the noble lord said, " Sure, sir, you do not think I would fire my pistol at you." He then carefully fired in the air.

This makes nonsense of his previous refusal to hand over his pistol on the grounds that he had not fired it, and, indeed, makes a farce of the whole proceedings. It is no wonder that all parties drew together to sort things out, and Lord Balcarres asked the routine question. Had Lord Shelburne any difficulty in declaring that he meant nothing personal to Colonel Fullarton?

His lordship immediately became prickly once more and replied, " You know it has taken another course. This is no time for explanation."

Lord Shelburne then turned to Colonel Fullarton and said politely, " Although I am wounded, I am able to go on if you feel any resentment."

Colonel Fullarton answered, " I hope I am incapable of harbouring such a sentiment."

A lesser man, outside the charmed circle, might have asked if that was so why the deuce the Colonel had provoked a duel. But Lord Frederick Cavendish had better manners than that. He solemnly declared, " From the character I have always heard of you, Colonel Fullarton, I believe that to be true."

Colonel Fullarton then said to Lord Shelburne, " As your lordship is wounded and has fired into the air, it is impossible for me to go on."

All parties must have been immensely relieved to hear that, because even their heads must have been going round in a bit of a fog, and Lord Balcarres and Lord Frederick Cavendish at once declared that the parties had ended the affair by behaving as men of the strictest honour.

After looking in upon such a scene we can only tiptoe away, full of confusion at having eavesdropped at an affair of such extreme delicacy, and slightly embarrassed at knowing little of what it has all been about.

Mr Donovan and Captain Hanson (1779)

That all duels were not so polite is shown by another in the previous year. Mr Donovan stopped Captain Hanson fighting another man, and the Captain gave him very abusive language and insisted that he " would make him smell powder."

The parties met in a field near the Dog and Duck at

Kingston, and even if Mr Donovan did have to smell powder it was Captain Hanson who received a bullet-wound in his body from which he died the next day. As usual, the abusive Captain Hanson changed the tune on his death-bed, and told the surgeons that Mr Donovan behaved during the action, and after it, with the greatest honour, tenderness, and concern. He particularly desired that no prosecution should be taken out against Donovan, as he himself was solely at fault by showing unprovoked rashness of temper and heat of passion.

Mr Donovan was tried for murder at Kingston Assizes. The Hon. Mr Justice Gould, in his charge to the jury, said, " I must inform the jury that, as for the idea of honour so often mentioned, it is false honour in men to break the laws of God and their country. In going out to fight a duel there is, in both parties, a deliberate resolution to commit murder, and there can be no honour in so savage a custom. . . ."

But the jury, without going out of court, acquitted Donovan of murder, and he was fined ten pounds for manslaughter, which he paid, and so was immediately discharged.

The Reverend Mr Allen and Lloyd Dulany, Esq., of Maryland, America (1782)

This quarrel arose out of the trouble between Great Britain and her colony of America, and was one of the journalistic duels that were quite common. The Reverend Mr Allen was a writer on the *Morning Post*, and Mr Dulany was an American of respectable character and much property. Allen wrote an article in the *Morning Post* in 1779 called " Characters of Principal Men of the

Rebellion," and when challenged by Dulany the writer made it clear that he intended to pin the charge of being a " liar and an assassin " upon Dulany's brother Daniel.

The outcome was inevitable. The parties met about half-past nine on a fine summer evening near Blackfriars, Allen not being deterred by the office he held. They fired at eight paces, and Dulany was shot, dying six days later.

It is noticeable that here are no fine speeches of forgiveness or high-flown compliments, and insults given by the pen have always seemed to produce exceptionally bad temper. A woman witness declared that she had seen the reverend gentleman shooting at a mark, or practising, in a field near Blackfriars Bridge on the very day of the duel. This was always considered very bad form, but Allen produced three witnesses to prove an alibi for that.

However, the parson came out of it rather worse than most, for at the Old Bailey, although only fined one shilling, he was sent to Newgate Prison for six months, which, with gaol fever rampant, was often equivalent to a death-sentence. There was perhaps an impression in the mind of the Recorder that such conduct was worse in a parson than in other men.

Lord Macartney and Major-General Stewart (1786)

This duel was fought near Kensington at 4.30 A.M. on June 8, 1786. The cause was never recorded. One of the seconds was the Colonel Fullarton we have seen in a model duel with the Earl of Shelburne. This duel has the same stamp about it.

The combatants took their ground at a distance of twelve short paces, but General Stewart told Lord Macartney that he doubted, as his lordship was short-

They fired at Eight Paces

sighted, whether he would be able to see him. His lordship replied, " I shall do perfectly well."

As the parties were about to raise their pistols General Stewart warned Lord Macartney that his pistol was not cocked. His lordship thanked him and cocked.

When they had levelled, General Stewart said, " I am ready." His lordship answered, " I am likewise ready." And they fired within a few seconds of each other.

Lord Macartney was hit in the chest, and, seeing this, the seconds said that the matter must rest there.

General Stewart said, " This is no satisfaction. Cannot his lordship fire another pistol? "

His lordship answered, " I will try, with pleasure. Do, I pray you, let me proceed, Fullarton."

But the seconds refused once more, and General Stewart said, " Then I must defer it to another occasion."

His lordship next made the following speech, which is remarkable when it is considered that he had to lean his back against a tree to stop himself falling from loss of blood.

" If that be the case we had better proceed now. I am here in consequence of a message from General Stewart, who called upon me to give him satisfaction in my private capacity for offence taken at public conduct. To show that personal safety is of no consequence to me, I have nothing personal. The General may proceed as he thinks fit."

The General answered, " It was your lordship's personal conduct to me that I resented."

He still wanted to go on, and Lord Macartney still wished to accommodate him. Both parties refused to quit their ground, but the seconds called up the surgeons, who were waiting at a distance. General Stewart then left the ground in company with his second, General Gordon, and an easy carriage was provided to convey his lordship home.

The Earl of Lonsdale and Captain Cuthbert of the Guards (1792)

There are many instances on record of metal buttons, watches, and coins in the pocket saving the lives of duellists. In 1826 an Irishman was on his way to adjust a little ' difficulty,' when he saw a horseshoe on the ground. With cries of joy he picked it up for luck and put it in his pocket. His opponent's bullet actually struck that horseshoe near his heart and glanced off harmlessly.

In 1814, during the ' Hundred Days,' when Napoleon escaped from Elba, two French Generals, Ornano and Bonnet, fought because Ornano received a promotion the other had expected. But besides losing his promotion General Bonnet came within a hundred-franc piece of losing his life. His opponent's bullet struck his watch-fob, in which he had a hundred-franc piece which deadened the shot. And the last laugh was with General Bonnet, because General Ornano was also wounded. He had to use crutches for two years, so missing the battle of Waterloo—although that may have been a blessing in disguise.

In 1787 a French Chevalier said that the " English Army had more solidity than spirit," which let him in for a duel with an English Captain. The parties were placed at the alarmingly short distance of five paces, and the Englishman's shot could hardly have failed to strike the Frenchman, which it did, on the breast. But by a miracle of good luck it was stopped by a metal button. The Chevalier was so overjoyed that he fired in the air and declared that the English have both spirit and solidity.

But probably the most famous duel of this kind occurred in England in 1792. There was rioting in the London streets, and Captain Cuthbert, on duty in Mount Street, had ordered that no carriage should pass along that street. Lord Lonsdale was stopped in his carriage, and, as he was not able to persuade his way through, his temper was " somewhat ruffled."

He therefore said to Captain Cuthbert, " You rascal, do you know that I am a peer of the realm? " The Captain immediately answered, " I don't know that you are a peer, but I do know you are a scoundrel for applying such a term to an officer on duty, and I will make you answer for it."

Naturally a meeting took place. Each man fired twice without effect, but Lord Lonsdale's second shot would have proved fatal if the ball had not struck a metal button of Captain Cuthbert's coat.

The seconds then interfered, and matters were amicably settled.

Robert Keon, Esq., and George Nugent Reynolds, Esq. (1788)

In January 1788 two Irish gentlemen went out to fight a duel in Dublin. Before they took off their coats Mr Reynolds, hat in hand, was in the act of wishing Mr Keon a good-morning when the latter fired his pistol and shot him through the head, killing him instantly.

Upon this Mr Plunket, Mr Reynolds' second, called out, " A horrid murder! " At which Mr Keon's brother replied, " If you don't like it, take that," and snapped his pistol at Mr Plunket, but luckily it did not go off.

What Colonel Fullarton and the Earl of Shelburne and Lord Frederick Cavendish would have said to such conduct passes imagination. But if they did hear of the case they must have been immensely gratified to know that Mr Plunket made a quick exit after he had been shot at, so that he was able to appear as a witness at Keon's trial for murder, and the Irish jury found the accused guilty of murder. Despite lawyers' tricks sentence of death was passed and executed without delay.

H.R.H. Frederick Augustus, Duke of York, and Captain Lennox (1789)

Little that is good is ever said of King George III and his sons, but at least it can be said that his second son had the courage to receive his opponent's fire in a duel and not return it.

The trouble started with a remark of the Duke of York's that " Captain Lennox had heard words spoken to him at Daubigny's Club to which no gentleman ought to have submitted."

When this was repeated to Captain Lennox he was so upset that as soon as he saw the Prince, which happened to be when His Royal Highness was inspecting the Coldstream Guards, he demanded to know what the words were and who had uttered them. His Royal Highness very properly gave no other answer than by ordering Captain Lennox back to his post on parade.

The parade over, His Royal Highness sent for the Captain and said, " I desire to derive no protection from my rank as a prince of the royal blood and my station as commanding officer. When not on duty, I wear a brown coat and am ready, as a private gentleman, to give you satisfaction."

After that interview the Captain sent a circular letter to every member of Daubigny's Club, asking if any of them had heard offensive words used to him. Nobody told him of such words, and the Captain then wrote to the Duke, pointing out the step he had taken and asking His Royal Highness to contradict the report as publicly as he had asserted it.

The Duke of York's answer was not satisfactory, and the Captain sent his second, the Earl of Winchilsea, to arrange a meeting. It took place that same evening, May 17, 1789, on Wimbledon Common, and Lord Rawdon was the Duke's second.

That the duel was fought in earnest is shown by the fact that Captain Lennox's bullet cut off a curl of His Royal Highness's hair, although one chronicler says that was impossible. He does not say whether that was because the Duke was bald or because his hair was straight. At any rate, it is beyond quibble that the Duke of York fired in the air and so brought the duel to an end.

Captain Lennox afterwards asked a jury of his fellow-officers to decide whether he had acted properly. Their decision was that " Captain Lennox has behaved with courage, but from the peculiar difficulty of his situation not with judgment."

Taking the hint, Captain Lennox soon after exchanged from the Coldstream Guards into the 35th Regiment of Foot, but his promotion was not affected. He later became Duke of Richmond and one of the most popular

The Duke of York fired in the Air

From a contemporary print

(Mansell Collection)

Viceroys Ireland ever had. The Irish would naturally welcome a man who had shot a curl off a British prince's head!

Sir George Ramsay and Captain Macrae (1790)

This is an excellent example of a fine man losing his life because of a pettifogging point of procedure.

Towards the close of the eighteenth century one of the wealthiest and most fashionable men in Edinburgh was Captain John Macrae. A handsome man, a fine amateur actor, he was amiable and generous, but he had one fault—a fierce temper he could not control.

Sir George Ramsay, of Banff, had just returned from India with an addition to his fortune and a recently married and beautiful wife, the sister of Lord Saltoun. He planned to settle down in his native country near all his friends. Sir George and his wife were regular attendants at Captain Macrae's private theatricals, and Sir George was well known as a gentleman of the most amiable character, a man loved by all.

On the evening of April 7, 1790, Captain Macrae escorted a lady out of the Edinburgh Theatre, and, seeing two men with a sedan-chair, he asked if they were engaged. They said they were not, but as the Captain was handing the lady into the chair a footman rushed out, seized one of the poles, and said that the chair was engaged for his mistress.

As he would not let go, Captain Macrae rapped his knuckles with a short cane, upon which the man struck the Captain and called him a scoundrel. One account says that the man was drunk, and that seems very likely. A passionate man like Captain Macrae could not take that sort of conduct, and he immediately gave the footman a thrashing.

When he knew it was Lady Ramsay's servant, Captain Macrae came into town and apologized at once. He first met Sir George, who said that the footman had been with them only a short time, and that, as he was Lady Ramsay's servant, he felt it was nothing to do with him.

There the matter would probably have ended, but James Merry, the footman, served a summons for assault on the Captain. Captain Macrae immediately wrote to Sir George to say that he must now demand the dismissal of the footman unless the prosecution was dropped.

It was a somewhat brusque note, which ended by saying: " As to his being Lady Ramsay's servant, it is of no consequence to me; I consider you as the master of your family and expect what I have now demanded shall be complied with."

This does rather sound as if Captain Macrae feared a prosecution, and perhaps we have not got the full facts of the quarrel with the footman. Sir George answered mildly that he hoped Captain Macrae would not make him interfere, especially as the man was far from well. But that evening, with indecent haste, a Captain Amory called on Sir George, and a duel was arranged for the next day at noon at Ward's Inn, near Musselburgh Links.

Sir George had Sir William Maxwell for his second, while Captain Amory attended upon Captain Macrae. Unfortunately a Captain Haig was also present to give his advice on the proper procedure for duelling.

Sir George, at any rate, showed no desire to blunder in. He made the handsome suggestion, through his second, that if Captain Macrae would apologize for the sharp tone of his letters the servant would be discharged.

But their adviser on etiquette, Captain Haig, would not hear of this. He said, " It is quite impossible. Sir George Ramsay must in the first place discharge his servant, and then Captain Macrae will apologize."

Captain Macrae is said to have burst into tears at this, and such pompous idiocy is enough to bring tears from a statue. But it was Lady Ramsay who should have been shedding the tears, for Captain Haig's ruling was meekly followed, and Sir George fell with a wound in the body of which he died two days later.

Captain Macrae was overcome with sorrow at seeing Sir George fall, and his seconds had difficulty in persuading him to leave the field. Acting on the advice of his solicitor, Captain Macrae and his second fled to France. As he did not surrender for trial, he was sentenced to outlawry. He lived for thirty years after that, but it was said that he was never the same man again. Far away from friends, home, and country, he passed a remorseful and miserable life until he died on January 16, 1820. What happened to Captain Haig is not recorded.

Mr Stephens and Mr Anderson (1790)

This duel was fought for perhaps the most trifling of all reasons: the two men argued about the shutting of a window in the public rooms at Margate. Mr Stephens, son of the Secretary to the Admiralty, was shot dead. Anderson was tried, but found guilty only of manslaughter. He was accused of murder, but the grand jury at Dover unanimously threw that charge out as " frivolous and unfounded."

Mr Graham, the Eminent Special Pleader, and Mr Julius (1791)

Mr Graham of the Temple, a leading special pleader of the day, presumably a barrister, found himself dining at the house of Mr Black in Epping Forest. In the company was Mr Julius, a law student, who expressed some free opinions about the existence of God which much annoyed Mr Graham. The argument was sharp, Mr Graham taking an orthodox view of religion.

They returned to town in the same carriage without fighting, but the argument was renewed the following Monday, and next day Mr Graham decided to use that eminently Christian weapon, the pistol, to prove to Mr Julius the error of his pagan thoughts.

But things did not work out as Mr Graham expected. They fought on Blackheath on July 19, 1791, in due form, with seconds and pistols and an eminent surgeon in attendance. Mr Graham was shot in the stomach, and, despite expert attention while he was hurried to town in a post-chaise, he died the next day.

We are not told of any sequel, although it is remarked that Mr Julius was not in any way to blame, and we do not know if he revised his beliefs about the existence of God after this incident.

Mr Frizell and Mr Clark, Law Students (1792)

It is to be hoped that Mr Graham's case did not set a bad example, but before a year was out two law students had fought a duel. The argument was far from being about religion, and the whole story reads like a scene from Dickens.

The two students were drinking in company with two friends at the Cecil Street coffee-house, where Mr Frizell lodged. They drank until one in the morning, when Mr Frizell said he could drink no more. Mr Clark took exception to this, accused Mr Frizell of being quarrelsome, and said he believed he had the reputation of a fighting man. Mr Frizell said he did not mean to give offence, but if anything he had said could be so construed he was ready to give Mr Clark satisfaction. He then went up to bed.

Clark insisted that the words were a direct challenge, and, although his friends said they were not of that opinion, he went up to Frizell's room and insisted that they should fight a duel in five minutes. Frizell dressed himself and came down, when he said that if their friends thought he had been guilty of any improper conduct he would apologize to Clark. But that gentleman said he would " accept of no apology," and insisted that they should fight in Hyde Park in an hour, at three o'clock.

Clark provided the pistols and, observing that Frizell had not got pistols, handed over one of his. They tossed up for the first fire, and against all justice Clark won. Worse still, Clark's first shot struck Frizell, and he fell.

One of the seconds ran off for a coach to take him to a surgeon, but on his return with the coach he found that Frizell was dead. Clark and his second were standing by the body, detained by some soldiers from Knightsbridge Barracks. The sergeant ran to ask his officer what was to be done, and was ordered to set the law students at liberty.

The body was put into the coach, into which they all got, but in Piccadilly, Clark and his second prudently got out and were not heard of in London again. All four students were Irish.

James Maitland, Eighth Earl of Lauderdale, and General
  Arnold (1791)

This duel is remarkable because the noble Earl was opposed to duelling and used passive resistance to express his disapproval.

Appropriately, the Earl's second was Charles James Fox, that mocker at duels. Lord Hawke, that famous cricketing name, was second to General Arnold. The meeting took place near Kilburn Wells, the cause being a misunderstanding which it was found impossible to conciliate.

Lord Lauderdale received the General's fire unhurt, but when he was asked to fire he said he did not come to fire at the General, nor could he apologize for the expressions he had used and which the General considered offensive. If General Arnold was not satisfied he might fire until he was!

This caused a rare flutter, and the seconds retired for ten minutes to consider the proper course, finally deciding to make the best of a bad job and call the matter off. This was doubtless considered very bad form on the part of the noble Earl.

The Right Hon. William Pitt and Mr George Tierney (1798)

This duel once more shows the social power of the duel, when the Prime Minister of England had to use a pistol to justify expressions he had used in the House of Commons! The meeting took place on Putney Heath, on May 27, 1798, at three in the afternoon. The parties stood at twelve paces, and both fired two pairs of pistols without effect. Pitt fired his second pistol in the air, and the seconds decided that sufficient satisfaction had been given and that the affair was ended with perfect honour on both sides.

England was in the doldrums at this time in her war with France, and such marksmanship from the Prime Minister was not a good example to his troops. But it is likely that the seconds had carefully loaded the pistols with insufficient powder so that the Prime Minister stood no chance of being shot—although they might have acted differently had they known that in December of the same year he was to introduce income tax in England!

Lieutenant-Colonel Montgomery and Captain Macnamara (1803)

On April 6, 1803, these two officers were riding in Hyde Park, each followed by a Newfoundland dog. The dogs fought, thus providing an excuse for a duel about as flimsy as that described by Shakespeare: " Thou hast quarrelled with a man for coughing in the street, because he hath wakened thy dog that hath lain asleep in the sun. . . ."

Captain Macnamara was a naval officer, about thirty-six years of age, strong, bold, and active. He was commander of a frigate, and had distinguished himself in several actions. He had already fought two or three duels.

Colonel Montgomery was Lieutenant-Colonel of the 9th Regiment of Foot, son of Sir William Montgomery of Ireland and half-brother to the Marchioness of Townshend. He was a remarkably handsome man and had fought bravely in Holland, in Egypt, and in Malta. He was very friendly with the Prince of Wales and the Duke of York.

When the two dogs went for each other Colonel Montgomery jumped from his horse and separated them.

Apparently not seeing Captain Macnamara, he angrily exclaimed, " Whose dog is that? I've a good mind to knock him down! "

Captain Macnamara thereupon jumped down from his horse, introduced himself, and said, " Have you the impudence to say you will knock my dog down? You will have first to knock me down! "

The combined military virtues and the social graces of the two officers completely failed to provide the obvious solution to such a ridiculous situation—a laugh and a handshake. Their good breeding had obviously produced a deficiency of brain; they could not even make the excuse that they were drunk.

Cards were solemnly exchanged, and the parties met at seven o'clock that same evening near Primrose Hill. They must have fought very close, fiendishly close, for both men fell at the first shot. Colonel Montgomery was carried into Chalk Farm, which was then still a farm, but later gave its name to the whole district. He died within five minutes.

Captain Macnamara was almost as badly wounded, but recovered to stand trial for murder at the Old Bailey.

His defence speech, prepared by Mr (later Lord) Erskine, declared: " I am a captain of the British Navy. To maintain that position, I must be respected. When called upon to lead others into honourable danger I must not be supposed to be a man who sought safety by submitting to what custom has taught others to consider a disgrace. . . . It is impossible to define in exact terms the proper feelings of a gentleman, but their existence has supported this country for many ages, and she might perish if they were lost."

Many spoke of Captain Macnamara's character, including Lords Hotham, Minto, Hood, and the immortal Nelson, but the Judge said that the jury " must find a verdict of manslaughter, at least."

The jury would have none of this. They evidently agreed that England depended on " the proper feelings of a gentleman," and that those feelings demanded the freedom to pistol anybody who insulted his dog, even if he happened to be another gentleman. They brought in a verdict of not guilty after a deliberation of only fifteen minutes.

Lord Camelford and Captain Best (1804)

The last Lord Camelford was a young man of two distinct personalities. In his public character he was a desperate ' bruiser ' and duellist. He was a nuisance to society, and sought quarrels on every possible occasion, and a writer of the day said he " died as he had lived, a bloodthirsty monster."

Yet another writer has said that he was a

man of superior abilities, but of singular character. . . . He was anxious to acquire knowledge of many things. He was a good chemist and mathematician, a most excellent geographer, a good seaman and he could do the work of a turner and cabinet-maker. He wished to be reckoned upon as a man independent of his title. But he desired to be at the head notwithstanding—to have the best horses and in points of dress and other things to be first.

That points to the kink in his character. Lord Camelford said himself that he believed he had been " born with no animal courage, and so laboured by any means to get the better of a weakness of nerves by attending cock-fighting, pugilism, and such-like."

That was the position in 1804. Camelford still had not proved to himself that he was not a coward, despite the duels and the fights he had been in. Then he heard that he was generally considered the second best pistol-shot in the kingdom. That would not do for Camelford: he must be the first. The fact that the first was his great friend, a Captain Best, could not be allowed to stand in the way.

The excuse happened to come very soon. A woman friend of Captain Best's made some proposal to him, which he refused. She said she would " set Lord Camelford upon him." She told Camelford that Captain Best had spoken disrespectfully of him.

Lord Camelford

Camelford marched up to Best at the Prince of Wales's coffee-house in Conduit Street, London, where they usually dined, and called out, " I find that you have spoken of me in the most unwarrantable terms."

Captain Best answered very mildly, but Camelford was not to be put off. He called Captain Best " a scoundrel, a liar, and a ruffian! "

A duel was inevitable, but Captain Best sent a message that evening to say that Lord Camelford was misinformed, and that if he would apologize for the terms he had used all would be forgotten. Camelford refused to listen, but even on the morning of the duel, when principals and seconds had met in a coffee-house in Oxford Street, Best made another effort.

He went up to his lordship and said, " Camelford, we have been friends for a long time, and I know the unsuspecting generosity of your nature. Upon my honour, you have been imposed upon by an abandoned woman. Do not persist in this course."

Lord Camelford replied, " Best, this is child's play. The affair must go on."

But the childishness came from the noble lord, who had to prove that he was the best pistol-shot in England or die.

The duel took place in a meadow to the west of Holland House, Kensington, where Melbury Road now runs. At fifteen paces the men faced each other, and Best, still reluctant to kill his friend, pointed his pistol wide. But Camelford cried, " That won't do! "

Camelford fired first, and came so close that Best heard the whistle of the shot. Best replied, and Camelford fell, shot in the chest and apparently dead. But he opened his eyes to say, " I am killed. But I acquit Best. I alone am to blame."

He advised Best to escape at once, which advice his friend took. Camelford lingered a couple of days, refusing to give the name of the gentleman who had shot him, saying that he was the aggressor, that he forgave his opponent, and that he hoped God would forgive him too.

But the man who wanted to prove he was so tough showed that he had a heart as sentimental as that of any Damon Runyon gangster. He left instructions that his body should be removed " to a country far distant—to a spot not near the haunts of men, but where the surrounding scenery may smile upon my remains."

The spot he indicated was on the borders of a lake in the canton of Bern, Switzerland, but even in that ambition Lord Camelford failed to achieve his ends. His body was embalmed and placed in a basket, but the Napoleonic Wars prevented its removal abroad. It was left in the crypt of St Anne's Church, Soho, and was finally lost, perhaps pushed into some forgotten vault or else stolen by body-snatchers, those men who sold bodies to surgeons for dissection.

Major Campbell and Captain Boyd (1808)

This is the third case to those already mentioned in which a British subject was sentenced to death for murder in a duel in modern times, and this is one of only two cases in which the sentence was carried out. The other was that of Robert Keon, which took place in 1788.

Major Alexander Campbell had seen service in several parts of the world, and particularly distinguished himself in Egypt, under Sir Ralph Abercromby. But when he was transferred to the 21st Fusiliers and promoted over the Senior Captain, Captain Boyd, Boyd showed his resentment, although it was certainly not the fault of the newcomer. Campbell was a hot-tempered man, and he was always being pin-pricked by the argumentative and disgruntled Boyd.

On June 23, 1808, the regiment had been reviewed, and in the mess that evening, in front of two other officers and Captain Boyd, Major Campbell remarked that General Kerr had corrected him about the way he gave an order, when he thought that he gave it correctly. Captain Boyd remarked, in what a witness later called a supercilious manner, that it was not correct according to the King's order. They argued for some time, until Captain Boyd said, " I know it better than you; you can take that as you wish."

Major Campbell got up and said, " Then, Captain Boyd, do you say that I am wrong? "

Boyd replied, " I do. I know I am right by the King's orders."

Major Campbell then quitted the room, Captain Boyd soon after followed him, and within twenty minutes Boyd was found in a room with a bullet-wound from which he died the next day.

When found, Campbell was still in the room, and a witness said he heard Campbell say, " On the word of a dying man, Boyd, was everything fair? " Boyd replied, " Campbell, you hurried me; you are a bad man." Campbell said again, " Boyd, before witnesses, was everything fair? " Boyd replied, " Oh my, Campbell, you know I wanted to wait and have seconds present! " Campbell insisted: " Good heavens, won't you mention before these gentlemen that everything was fair? Did you not say you were ready? " Boyd answered, " Yes," but soon after repeated, " Campbell, you are a bad man."

Boyd was helped into the next room, and Campbell followed, much agitated, and kept telling Boyd that he was the happier of the two of them. " I am an unfortunate man," Major Campbell declared, " but I hope not a bad one."

Major Campbell fled and lived at Chelsea under a false name, eluding the efforts of the authorities to catch him. He got tired of the hole-and-corner existence and gave himself up, to be tried for the murder of Captain Boyd at Armagh Assizes.

His defence was his character for humanity, peaceable conduct, and proper behaviour. Many officers testified to this, but the jury brought in a verdict of guilty of murder.

It was a surprising verdict considering the habit of juries in those days, and it is thought that Campbell helped to bring it about when he said that surely the verdict could not be murder, but must be manslaughter. One of the defence witnesses also had an unfortunate and condescending manner, as if to say, " I am appearing to speak for the defendant; surely that should be enough to acquit him! "

Even more surprisingly, the execution was carried out, and the prisoner's request to be shot and not hanged was refused, although he was first cousin to the Earl of Breadalbane. Campbell met death with the courage of a soldier and, it was said, the resignation of a Christian. He could have escaped from gaol, but refused because that would have meant getting his gaoler into trouble.

His poor wife travelled to London under great difficulties to petition the King, helped on her way by some humble fishermen who risked their lives to get her across the Irish Sea. The King had gone to bed, but the Queen saw Mrs Campbell, and, indeed, she received the kindest attention from all the royal family.

Mrs Campbell left the palace still hoping that her husband would be reprieved, but she reached Ayr, her father's home, on the very morning that her husband's corpse was brought there to be buried.

Lord Castlereagh and George Canning (1809)

Here are two more people often met in school history-books, and this duel might have set a fashion that would have had its advantages. Many would say that if there is one group of men who might be allowed to fight duels against each other it is the politicians.

Castlereagh's complaint was that, both he and Canning being members of the Prime Minister's Cabinet, Canning had worked secretly to get Castlereagh removed from the post of Secretary for War. On the surface it seemed to Castlereagh that his colleagues were working with him, whereas in fact they were working against him. In his written challenge Castlereagh said, " You know I *was* deceived and you *continued* to deceive me."

If this were true Canning's conduct was wrong, both as a statesman and a gentleman. To continue to act with a Minister whose removal he had urged on the plea of incompetence was most dishonourable. But it is hard to see how a duel could alter matters. A duel presupposes an injury done to ' honour,' and in this case Canning had injured only his own honour.

The meeting took place on September 21, 1809, in the early morning, on Putney Heath. Lord Yarmouth was Lord Castlereagh's second, and Canning was accompanied by Mr Ellis. They fired at ten yards, and both missed. No apology being offered, they fired again, and this time Canning was wounded in the left thigh, but it was only a flesh wound, not dangerous. He was put into a coach and taken to Gloucester Lodge, his newly purchased seat at Brompton, near Hyde Park, and Lord Castlereagh returned to his house in St James's Square, London.

It is noticeable that these politicians did not waste time making polite speeches to each other, and there is no mention of tenderness or solicitude for the wounded man.

George Payne, Esq., and Mr Clarke (1810)

The supporters of duelling often claimed that one good reason for duelling was that defenceless women had to be defended.

George Payne had been left a handy fortune of £14,000 a year, which would be a very large amount in modern money. He was married, with four children, but unfortunately for him an orphan daughter of Dr Clarke of Newcastle was a friend of Mrs Payne's and a regular visitor to the house. Mr Payne showed Miss Clarke some attention, and her brother decided that those attentions went beyond what was necessary in a host, even a host with £14,000 a year, and he challenged Mr Payne to a duel.

The challenge was given at Scarborough, where Mr Payne lived, but the men travelled to London to fight, possibly because Miss Clarke had no desire to be protected. On a September morning of 1810, at 5.30 A.M., three post-chaises were seen passing over Putney Bridge carrying the two principals and their seconds to fight the duel on Wimbledon Common.

Within an hour one of the chaises returned to the Red

Lion at Putney, bearing Mr Payne, mortally wounded with a shot in the groin. He died at 4.30 P.M. the same day. Mr Clarke made his escape, no doubt feeling satisfied that he had done his duty as a brother. But Mrs Payne and her four children and his own sister possibly had very different views on the matter.

Major Hillas and Mr Thomas Fenton (1815)

Towards the end of December in the year of Waterloo a duel took place in unusual circumstances in Ireland.

On a dark, stormy night a vessel was driven ashore upon the Irish coast, near Tireragh, close to the house of Major Hillas, an active magistrate and known far and wide as a kind-hearted and earnest man. He hurried to the wreck, and, finding that the captain had been drowned and that the mate and crew of eleven were at sixes and sevens, he took charge. Because of his exertions the crew and the cargo were saved.

In the midst of the struggle a neighbouring gentleman, Mr John Fenton, came up and without any cause for interfering did so in a rude and overbearing manner. Major Hillas naturally resented this, and threatened that if Mr Fenton did not immediately leave the ship he would throw him overboard.

Mr Fenton went off at this, and Major Hillas continued to work on the vessel from the 6th to the 8th of December. Mr Fenton then returned with a party of yeomanry and took the cargo out of the Major's hands in order to claim salvage on what had been saved. It is hard to understand why the yeomanry should have obeyed Fenton's orders against a man who was a magistrate, but obey him they did.

Major Hillas protested, and said that he was saving the cargo not for himself, but for the owners. Fenton would not listen, and Major Hillas took the trouble to travel to Scotland to inform the owners of what was going on. Fenton knew of this, and sent Major Hillas a challenge as soon as he returned, but the Major refused to accept any challenge until there had been an investigation.

The investigation took place, but four days afterwards, before its findings were known, John Fenton delivered a challenge from his brother, Thomas Fenton. What this brother had to do with it or why the Major accepted his challenge we are not told, but he did accept it.

When he arrived at the appointed place a large crowd had assembled to see the so-called sport. Major Hillas addressed the crowd as follows: " I am sorry that the mistaken laws of honour oblige me to come here to defend myself, and I declare to God I have no animosity to man or woman on the face of the earth."

Major Hillas seemed to have a premonition of the fatal result, for he had dressed himself in a full suit of mourning. He was shot dead at the first fire, and although Fenton was tried for murder, he was acquitted by the jury. This is, perhaps, not surprising when you have a magistrate who knows that duelling is a " mistaken law of honour " and yet does not have the moral courage to refuse to take part in it.

Captain Stackpole and Lieutenant Cecil (1814)

This shows how an insult can be kept in storage for four years and yet lose nothing of its potency.

In 1810 an officer asked Lieutenant Cecil if he knew Captain Stackpole, commander of the frigate *Statira*. Cecil replied that he knew Stackpole for a brave officer, but believed him capable of occasionally " drawing a long bow." Stackpole heard of this, and declared that he would call Cecil to account whenever they met.

Now, Stackpole was a crack pistol-shot, the best in the Navy, and it would have seemed fortunate for Cecil that they did not meet for four years. But in 1814 the *Statira* was lying in Port Royal, Jamaica, when the *Argo* entered that port. Captain Stackpole knew that Cecil was lieutenant in the *Argo*, and he at once sent a message saying that they must meet or Cecil must make a public apology for the phrase he had used.

Cecil answered that four years had gone by, and he could not remember how far his words had been reported correctly, but as a brother-officer had quoted them he would not argue. As for apologizing, he would apologize to any other officer in the Navy, but not to Captain Stackpole.

This was because of Stackpole's reputation as a crack shot: Cecil believed that people would say he was afraid to fight. Stackpole had been the friend and companion of Lord Camelford, and had almost as great a reputation as a shot, while Cecil seems to have acquired Camelford's fear of being thought a coward.

But the result of the duel was unexpected—particularly to Captain Stackpole. Stackpole fired first and actually missed. This so surprised the gallant officer that when Lieutenant Cecil's bullet hit him all he could say was, " By George, I've missed him! " He died almost immediately.

The Duke of Wellington and the Earl of Winchilsea (1829)

It is perhaps as well to end this section on the highest note, and it is almost impossible to speak of the first half of the nineteenth century without bringing in the Duke of Wellington. But even in 1829 many people must have realized that this duel showed that duelling would soon be on its last legs.

Briefly, the Duke of Wellington was bringing in an overdue measure of simple justice, the Roman Catholic Relief Bill, to which the Earl of Winchilsea was opposed. The Earl was one of the diehard ' No Popery ' men left over from the previous century. He chose to attack Wellington, who was sponsoring the establishment of King's College, London University, by saying that the Duke did this only so that he might pose as a good Protestant when he intended to let loose the Roman Catholics.

The letter was published in the *Standard*, and Wellington at once wrote to Winchilsea to inquire his motives. Many letters passed, and finally the parties agreed to fight a duel in Battersea Fields.

But even the Earl of Winchilsea's own second agreed to act only if the Earl promised not to fire at the Duke! Lord Falmouth, the second in question, thought that the Earl had offended so badly that an apology was not enough: he must receive the Duke's fire without returning it.

The Duke, seeing that the Earl kept his pistol pointing at the ground, fired at random. The Earl's second then delivered a written apology, on which the Duke asked that one word should be pencilled in. Wellington then said he was satisfied so long as the apology was published in the *Standard*. This the Earl promised to have done, and all parties gravely retired, honour satisfied.

Gilbert and Sullivan's comic operas came some forty years later, and it needs their talent to do justice to such a scene. But the significant thing is that the newspapers of the day realized the absurdity of such affairs and poked fun. Although juries were still stolidly bringing in verdicts of not guilty in trials for murder by duelling, when people begin to laugh at an institution meant to be serious, then its days are numbered.

The following account of the duel is taken from the *Morning Herald* of March 23, 1829:

> The City was thrown into ferment this morning by a report which seemed so utterly improbable that at first few believed it. . . . We were among the incredulous, thinking it a story fit only to amuse male and female old ladies—those gossippers in and out of petticoats. But every third person we met told us seriously how His Grace the Duke of Wellington had taken offence at his lordship's, the Earl of Winchilsea's, letter about the King's College; how the aforesaid noble Duke had challenged the aforesaid noble Earl; how the said noble belligerents had agreed to meet, stand up, and fire at one another at the distance of twelve paces, like sage statesmen and true Christians; how they accordingly did meet this morning in Battersea Fields among the cabbages; how his Grace, the Prime Minister of England, shot at his lordship, the Earl of Winchilsea . . . how, thereupon, the noble Earl fired his pistol in the air; how the Earl's second presented a written apology and so the affair was amicably settled. . . .

> Yes, reader, it was true. The Duke of Wellington, the first warrior of his day, the conqueror of Napoleon, the Prime Minister of England and the author of a law which he says

is necessary for the welfare of the Empire, placed himself in a situation where he might have been charged with murder . . . merely because a noble lord wrote a pettish letter, which even his best friends laughed at. No wonder the multitude break laws when the law-makers themselves, the great, the powerful, and the famous, set them at open defiance.

The noble lords wished each other good-morning and returned to town. About fifteen gardeners and labouring men, who were on the spot during the transaction, advised the noble combatants to settle the matter in dispute with their fists.

(c) AFTER 1837

Eccentric Duels in the Nineteenth Century

From the 1830s duelling slackened off in Great Britain. The last duel recorded as being fought by a British subject took place in 1862 between a Mr Dillon and the Duc de Grammont-Cadérousse, in which Mr Dillon was killed.

In this period, too, came most of the eccentric duels. For example, in 1808, two Frenchmen quarrelled over an opera dancer. Being of ' elevated minds,' they fought in balloons high over Paris. One was shot down and, with his second, was killed. In 1843 two Frenchmen fought with red billiard balls, and one threw so accurately that he killed his opponent outright. Then there were two other Frenchmen who duelled on and off for nineteen years.

Duelling persists longer in Latin Countries

In fact, it is perhaps surprising that duelling persisted in France much longer than it did in England. That nation, famed for its logic and reasoning powers, saw nothing illogical in the duel of honour. Towards the end of the last century the well-known Parisian newspaper *L'Evènement* stated: " In France everybody fights, or is liable to fight, and no one thinks of contesting the legitimacy of duelling. Duelling renders more service to social order than a police magistrate. It purges offences better than legal proceedings, which often leave a nasty taste in the mouth. . . ." Legislative assemblies, politicians, and lawyers defended the duel, and one famous lawyer, Jules Janin, said, " I would not consent to live twenty-four hours in society, such as it is at present, if duelling did not exist."

But perhaps French logic did show itself in that the French duellist was often not terribly in earnest—like the renowned literary critic Sainte-Beuve, who insisted on fighting a duel with pistols from under his umbrella, declaring that he was quite ready to be killed, but he did not wish to catch cold. The duel was seldom fought to the death—to draw blood was sufficient—and its conduct was so hedged about with rules and etiquette that, despite the vast numbers of disputes settled in this way in the last century, few duellists were killed. The majority of duellists were found among young men about town, journalists, and politicians.

The Breittmayer–Lusciez Affair
A photograph of the actual duel
(Mansell Collection)

Yet the fact remains that duels were fought in France and Italy throughout the nineteenth century and well into this century. In 1878 Gambetta, a famous politician, called another Deputy a liar, and so had to fight a serious duel. In 1898, at Rome, Signor Felice Cavallotti, an Italian Deputy, was killed in a duel with Signor Macola, the leader of the Extreme Radical Party. As late as December 31, 1905, a fierce duel in Paris between two accomplished swordsmen, M. Georges Breittmayer and M. Armand Lusciez, lasted nearly two hours, until wounds and fatigue stopped a determined effort to fight to the death.

Thus it is a fact that the habit of duelling persisted in France, often called the most civilized of countries, some seventy years longer than it did in England. But the idea of honour compelling a man to accept any challenge, no matter how foolish or malicious or one-sided, was strictly maintained in the British armed forces long after our civilians had somewhat shamefacedly abandoned the notion. In the twenty-five years between 1837 and 1862 practically all British duels were fought by officers of the Army or the Navy, and most of them on foreign stations.

It is proposed to describe only one such duel, and that at some length, for the pathetic case of Ensign Sarsfield perfectly sums up the evils of the duelling code of honour.

The Case of Ensign Sarsfield (1842)

The chronicler of this affair, William Douglas, himself an Army officer, altered the names of the men concerned, but he vouches for the truth of the story.

In the year 1842 Her Majesty Queen Victoria's 173rd Regiment of Foot was stationed at Poona, in India, one of the best stations in the Bombay Presidency for health, pleasure, and good society. But daily life was dull, enlivened only by balls, cricket matches, races, and regimental sports. Even the half-yearly inspection by the commanding General was regarded as an event.

Poona was at one time a byword for snobbery. Even in 1842 there was plenty of it. The Queen's officers looked down upon their brethren in the East India Company's regiments, and both looked down upon the officers of native infantry corps. There were also other divisions affecting status, such as the school an officer had attended, his nationality, his religion, or the number of duels he had fought.

The 173rd Regiment of Foot were mostly Irish 'Orangemen,' or Protestants, so that Catholics usually had a bad time of it in that regiment. It happened that in 1842 an ensign we will call Sarsfield, son of a noble Irish family and a Catholic, was drafted from a home station to join the Regiment.

Sarsfield soon found that he was not welcome and that his appointment to the 173rd was looked upon as an impertinence, although he had had no say in it. If Sarsfield had been a crack shot or a cricketer or an athlete, or even able to sing a rowdy comic song, things might have been different. But he was a timid, bashful boy, slight of figure and with a refined, thoughtful cast of countenance that his fellow-officers soon dubbed 'girlish.'

He found himself thrown almost entirely on his own company, and, as so often happens in a hot climate, he began to drink more than was good for him. He was in no sense a drunkard. It was simply that his capacity for drink was small, and he often found himself with nothing to do and the brandy-pawnee at his elbow.

It happened at mess one night, after a cricket match in which the regimental eleven had been beaten, that Sarsfield spoke out of turn. Like most shy people who have drunk a glass too many, from having too little to say, Sarsfield was apt to talk too much. In the course of the cricket discussion Sarsfield doubted an assertion made by one of the players of the same rank as himself, a Lieutenant Craigsfoot.

" Do you mean to say I'm a liar? " shouted Lieutenant Craigsfoot.

Sarsfield nodded and stretched out his hand for another glass.

A silence fell on the room. Craigsfoot rose up in offended majesty, bowed to Sarsfield, and left the mess, followed by the paymaster and the other officers, one after the other.

The brandy was so powerful that even then Sarsfield did not seem to realize his offence and its consequences. He coolly drank some more brandy-pawnee and then went home to bed.

He was awakened at four o'clock the next morning by the paymaster, who came with a message from Lieutenant Craigsfoot demanding satisfaction for the insult or an apology. Sarsfield, in his right senses and genuinely sorry for what he had said in the heat of wine, at once said he would apologize and signed a document without looking at it.

Sarsfield was only eighteen years of age, and at the depot at home he had been told that anybody who fought a duel would be court-martialled. Worse still, he had nobody to turn to for advice, although they could only have told him that to apologize would be as good as admitting that he was a coward. Sarsfield therefore signed the abject apology and went to sleep again.

There was a parade at 6 A.M. that morning, and Sarsfield, without the least idea that he had disgraced himself, walked across to join a group of brother-officers. To his astonishment, his good-morning was met by a cold stare from each one, and, turning their backs, they walked away. At first it did not occur to Sarsfield that this was because he had apologized instead of fighting.

Poor Sarsfield led a dog's life in the next three months. He had to appear on all parades, attend the orderly-room as required, and perform the usual regimental duties. But in all that time not one of the other officers would speak one word to him unless it was necessary in the course of duty.

But the men were all on his side, and his batman idolized him. Even that was turned against him, for it was said that he made companions of private soldiers by asking them to his bungalow to drink and talk, which would have been hardly surprising in the circumstances.

Even if Sarsfield had transferred to another corps his reputation as a coward would have travelled with him, and so the lonely boy had to drift down his private stream of misery without a single friend to advise him to apply for a transfer home or else to leave the service.

Those who should have been his friends were cruelly waiting to see if he would commit suicide or shoot one of his tormentors, and at last their curiosity was satisfied.

For a long time Sarsfield had not gone to mess, having his food sent to his bungalow, but one night, to the surprise of his batman, he said that he would dine in mess. The batman said he hoped everything would come right.

Sarsfield answered, " Yes, everything will be right by to-morrow at this time."

When he entered the mess-room conversation ceased

and a meaningful glance passed round the table. There was a vacant seat right opposite the paymaster, which Sarsfield took.

Now, the paymaster was known to be the crack shot of the regiment who had already fought successfully in half a dozen duels, and the reason for Sarsfield's choice of that seat was soon obvious.

Sarsfield's brother-officers resumed their conversations, but nobody took the slightest notice of him, either by word or look. He was waited upon by the servants the same as the others, and it was just as the table had been cleared for the second course that everybody heard Sarsfield, in a clear and firm voice, ask the paymaster to take wine with him.

" I do not take wine with a coward," the paymaster said.

" But you will take this," Sarsfield answered, as he flung the wine-glass and its contents in the paymaster's face.

In an instant all was uproar, and Sarsfield was pulled from the mess-room into the anteroom. Now that his life was numbered in minutes, other officers were ready to speak to him, even to speak kindly.

The doctor, himself reckoned the third best duellist in the corps, said, in a voice that might almost have been sorrowful, " My boy, you will have to fight now."

" I know that well enough," Sarsfield answered. " I came for that purpose."

It was a beautiful moonlit tropical night, and half an hour's walk brought principals, doctor, and seconds to the Parsee's Garden, where Poona affairs of honour were settled. What young Sarsfield thought about on that walk is, of course, not recorded.

All was now done with strict fairness. The formalities were carefully observed, and the captain of his company even acted as Sarsfield's second, but this meant no more than acting as a coffin-bearer.

The result was never in doubt. Sarsfield fell dead, shot through the heart, his own pistol unfired.

The corpse was placed in a palanquin and hurried to the dead boy's bungalow, where his servant was told to prepare the body for burial. The poor fellow was overcome with grief, but he did what was asked, promised secrecy, and was sent back to his own barrack-room.

The next issue of the *Poona Gazette* printed, among its Notices of Death, the following: " Suddenly of cholera, in the officers' lines of Her Majesty's 173rd Light Infantry, Ensign J. S. Sarsfield."

I

THE DUEL AT ITS HEIGHT

No account of duelling among the English-speaking
peoples could pretend to be complete without reference
to our cousins in the States. There duelling was, in the
nineteenth century, a very serious business, especially
in the South. Duels were often fought with three weapons
—pistols, rifles, and bowie-knives—and sometimes with
specially grown finger-nails as auxiliary weapons! And
the custom persisted in outlandish parts even as late as
1917.

Andrew Steinmetz, writing in 1868, six years after an
Englishman last fought in a duel, said:

> In most countries, the duel is a sort of offhand polite
> diversion. But in the States men fight in earnest. Revolvers
> are ever revolving. No objection to fowling-pieces, to rifles,
> to bowie-knives. Put up your hand to scratch the back of
> your neck and the man nearest you will whip out a bowie-
> knife. The walls of hotel bedrooms, even in Washington,
> the capital, are riddled with bullet-holes. . . . The bar-
> tender always has a revolver on the shelf behind him.

There is no doubt that duels in the States were more
ferocious and more frequently fatal than anywhere else
in the world. It was against this background that Benjamin Franklin, America's own philosopher, tried to

make the voice of common sense heard. His words are quoted at the beginning of this book.

(a) THE COLONIAL PERIOD

When America was a colony of England, between the arrival of the Pilgrim Fathers and 1775, " when bad King George couldn't rest in his bed," there was little duelling. The Puritans and the Quakers and the Dutch of New York outlawed it on religious grounds. The elegant English gentlemen who founded Jamestown under Captain John Smith had their hands full in keeping alive (although they did try to assassinate Captain Smith).

Peter de Lancey and Dr Haly (1770)

But as 1775 and the break with England approached, duelling had begun to creep in. The most famous duel took place in 1770, when Peter de Lancey, Deputy Postmaster of North America, fought his friend Dr Haly, an Irish doctor. De Lancey supported George III's party, but the cause of the quarrel is unknown. The gentlemen had dinner together, apparently without quarrelling, but afterwards they went to a tavern, hired a room, called for candles and wine, bolted the shutters, and sent the waiter away. Shouts were heard, and De Lancey was found dying with a ball in his left side. Dr Haly had rushed out to find a doctor, the smoking pistol still in his hand, as it was considered wrong for a doctor to attend any man he had shot. Dr Haly was charged and found guilty of manslaughter, but suffered no penalty. There were no seconds present, and in this respect and in other circumstances this duel was remarkably like that between Mr Chaworth and Lord Byron already described, which took place in England five years earlier, in 1765.

The Laurens Family

But the ' code of honour ' was strong in the South, where even opponents of duelling could not escape involvement. Henry Laurens, an important citizen of Charleston, was one such anti-duellist. He took the field, risked being killed by his opponent's fire, and directed his own shot deliberately wide. Laurens warned his own son, John, against duelling, but in 1778 John seriously wounded General Charles Lee in a duel because he spoke slightingly of George Washington, who, incidentally, always opposed duelling.

(b) THE EARLY YEARS OF THE REPUBLIC

As in England, any gentleman or officer in America who refused a challenge was branded a coward for ever more. The only exception was in New England, where duels were considered barbarous and even officers did not fight them.

You might colour the map of the States white from the northern border down to New York City. South of that you would shade it pinker and redder, until you came to the most sinister blood-red in Georgia and South Carolina.

Charleston and Savannah were the record-breaking cities for duels, and the ' code of honour ' was observed for so long in those parts that a gentleman had to pay it closer attention in 1870 than his ancestors had done in 1780!

Major James Jackson

Perhaps the fierceness of the Southern duel can best be seen in this episode from the career of Major Jackson, a politician who was not only fearless and aggressive, but honest as well.

The Creek Indians had been turned out of their valuable lands on the Yazoo river, and in 1791 a pretty little plot was hatched up by the Georgian politicians to buy their lands at 1½ cents an acre, for resale to the public at enormously inflated prices.

To fight this, Jackson transferred from the United States Senate to the Georgian, where he beat the crooked politicians after a hard struggle.

They were, of course, angry when their easy money vanished, and one of them, Robert Watkins, waited outside the State Capitol, then at Louisville, with a gang of friends to back him up.

Watkins coolly called Jackson a twisting rascal, and Jackson, not unnaturally, called Watkins a liar, backing his words with blows from a cane he carried. Next, he fired a pistol, but it was knocked up, and Watkins rushed at Jackson to stab him with a bayonet attached to his pistol. In the scuffle Watkins tried to gouge out Jackson's eye with his finger-nails. Jackson protected his eyes by getting his teeth in Watkins's fingers, but Watkins then stabbed with his bayonet and wounded Jackson seriously, at which the interested and applauding onlookers dragged them apart.

These men, it must be remembered, were leading citizens, not poor whites drunk on pay day. Usually men who called themselves gentlemen fought duels; the rest killed one another in street or tavern brawls. In country parts of Georgia strangers commented on the long finger-nails worn by the men and laughed uneasily when told that the nails were weapons—for gouging your opponent's eyes.

Not that duels were fought only in Georgia and South Carolina.

William Thornton and Francis Conway

In the Virginia of the early eighteen-hundreds these two young men were friends, although both courting the same girl, Nellie Madison, niece of a future President of the United States. A jest of Conway's about a Negro who had put Thornton's new saddle on Conway's horse was passed on by Nellie, making it look as if Conway had accused his friend of theft.

The two friends fought on Christmas Day, and each lodged a ball in the other. Thornton rode home, but next day both were dead.

The case became legendary because Conway's mother told at breakfast of a dream she had had that night in which a man had ridden up on a white horse to announce her son's death. When the very same man rode up that afternoon on the very same horse Mrs Conway knew the message he brought before he opened his mouth.

(c) BETWEEN 1800 AND 1850

The duel was at its height during this half-century. Among civilians, newspaper men and politicians were most frequently ' called out.' Even in New York, in the North, duels were sometimes fought, although they usually took place on the Jersey side of the Hudson river to avoid the law officers. The law of the land, as in England, forbade duelling, but in the South the law officers turned a blind eye, and judges often fought duels themselves.

The last duel in New York took place in 1804, when a

Republican politician, Captain Thompson, who was also Collector of the Port of New York, called William Coleman, editor of the New York *Evening Post*, a coward. To avoid the law, the meeting was timed for eleven at night in what is now University Place, New York City, but which was a country lane in 1803.

The duel was fought at eleven paces in a blinding snowstorm, and it is not surprising that both missed with the first two shots. At the third Captain Thompson dropped, crying, " I've got it! "

Surgeons and seconds swore to keep his death a secret, and, surprisingly, the vow was kept for a long time. Even when his post as Collector of the Port was advertised nothing was said of his death.

The Army and the Navy

The officers of the young Republic took themselves very seriously as officers and gentlemen, and although duelling was forbidden in the Army in 1806 (in the Navy not until 1862), it made no difference. They called each other out on the slightest provocation, and nobody was court-martialled. They even had official encouragement from one of the Presidents, Jackson, who publicly stated that, as officers followed the profession of arms, he believed it proper that they should shoot one another. If they did not, he declared, the fine edge of their courage might become dull and rusty.

The majority of the duels were between the lower ranks of officers, the younger ensigns and lieutenants, who had to strut and prove their bravery. Practically every Army post had its tombstone like the one to a young ensign named Wilde. It said:

He fell on 16th January, 1815, by the hand of a man who but for him would have been friendless, and expired instantly, in his 22nd year. He died, as he lived, with unshaken courage and unblemished reputation. By his untimely death, the prop of a Mother's age is broken, the hope and consolation of a Sister is destroyed, the pride of Brothers humbled in the dust, and a whole family, happy until then, overwhelmed with affliction.

Duels in the Navy, especially among the midshipmen, or ' reefers,' were even more frequent. Nerves became frayed in the crowded living quarters on long voyages, and the naval discipline was very harsh.

Everybody in the junior mess became very touchy, as can be seen from the affair of Decatur and Somers.

They were lieutenants in the undeclared war with France of 1800, and bosom pals, lifelong friends. On some trivial occasion Decatur laughingly called Somers a fool, and neither thought any more about it. But their mess-mates refused to drink with Somers because he had been called a fool and had not challenged to a duel, as behoved an ' officer and gentleman.'

" Hang it, he's my best friend! " cried Somers. " He spoke only in fun."

The others would not budge. Many duels had been fought between bosom friends, and even the offer of a dinner to the whole mess by Decatur made no difference.

In the end Somers said he would fight the lot of them rather than fight his friend. The others could hardly refuse, and next morning Somers faced them one after the other, with Decatur as his second.

Somers was shot twice in the first two duels, and became so weak from loss of blood that Decatur had to sit by him on the ground and hold up his pistol-arm. This time Somers wounded his opponent, and then the other officers called the whole thing off, declaring that Somers had proved his courage. It has truly been said that there is no animal so foolish as the human animal!

The fighting midshipmen were usually mere boys who often fought for reasons just as stupid as in the Decatur–Somers affair. Two midshipmen fought because one said the Queen of Russia was a good-looking woman and the *Empress* other said she was not; two others because one said a bottle was green and the other said it was black. Another had to fight because he happened to walk into the mess with his hat on; another met his death because he jokingly sprinkled water on his friend; two others fought because one wanted the scuttle open and the other preferred it shut. In the latter case they had not thought of fighting, but later a senior officer told them that language had been used which no officer and gentleman could over-look and still keep his honour. As a result of this elder's sage advice, the two friends fought, against their own wishes, and one was crippled for life.

The number of deaths from duelling in those fifty years will never be known, as the cause of death was often omitted from the records. It was rare for a tomb-stone to be explicit as the following:

> In Memory of William R. Nicholson, a midshipman in the Navy of the United States, who was cut off from Society in the bloom of his youth and health through an affair of honour on 18 September, 1804, aged 18 years.

The Effect of the Duel on ordinary Life

Despite the quick fading of the duel in the northern

states, the rest of the country paid no heed, and duelling reached a frenzy in the South and in the Western border states during the period from the eighteen-twenties to the eighteen-forties.

In the course of this book we have seen that everywhere it was in the leisured classes that duelling flourished. They ' civilized ' violence into the rigid rules and ritualistic combat of the duel.

Nowhere was this strange co-existence of gracious living and bloodshed more marked than in the Southern States of America. It is extraordinary how women encouraged duelling. They stood to lose their husbands, their sons, everything dear to them. In a young country like America the male breadwinner was even more important than in other communities, and yet women clung desperately to the idea of the duel. A famous doctor of Charleston, James Marion Sims, wrote: " I was educated to believe that duels were a pillar of society and that they protected the honour of women." This vague and woolly idea must have been in the minds of the Southern ladies as they watched their dead husbands and sons being carried solemnly into the house after paying a ' debt of honour.'

In fact, men seldom fought duels over women. Over a joke, a gambling debt, a newspaper attack, a refusal to drink, a political argument—any little thing, but hardly ever over a woman. Yet somehow it was generally believed as an indisputable proposition that if there were no duels no honest woman would be safe in the land.

And such a callous, foolish manner of behaving made the women as insensitive as the men. In 1843 a Dr Archer and one Otway Crump fell into argument. Archer was ready to apologize verbally for a remark he had made, but he would not publish an apology. Crump challenged, and Archer sent to Mrs Crump asking her to persuade Crump to be reasonable.

She only grinned, and Archer warned her that he had done all he could, and more.

" If we meet I shall shoot your husband through the heart, madam."

" Oh, well, he'll have to take his chance of that, won't he ? " Mrs Crump answered.

Soon after Mr Crump was duly carried home on a door with a bullet through his heart.

Young People and the Duel. The same brutalizing effect could be seen in the children who were allowed to watch duels and public hangings. When Governor Robert Wright met Governor Lloyd, Wright took his twelve-year-old son as his second.

It was arranged that the two men should walk towards each other and fire when they chose. Wright fired first and missed. Lloyd still held his fire, and they came face to face, Lloyd saying, " Your life, sir, is in my hands."

At which Wright's young son sang out, " Papa, tell him to shoot and be damned to him! "

Luckily the other man showed human compassion, or Wright junior would have been without a father. But the story is significant because it was quoted everywhere as an example of manly courage in childhood.

Negro Duellists

As in Europe, the duel was something by which you knew a gentleman, but Negro slaves sometimes emulated their masters. In one duel a Negro was killed and his opponent lay badly wounded for two days before he was found.

A Virginian gentleman remarked, " Depressed and debased as the Negroes are, they sometimes exhibit traits of character which elevate them above the sphere to which our policy compels us to confine them. The strict observance of honourable conduct and the cool, determined courage of the Negroes in this duel affords an example which ought to make some gentlemen of high position blush."

Newspapermen

Nowadays we think of a newsman's life as hectic, but not dangerous except in time of war. In the peaceful days of the mid-nineteenth century in the United States, however, editors had to be quick on the draw if they were to cheat death.

The record number of staff duellings must have been held by the *Sentinel* of Vicksburg. In 1838 its editor, one Hagan, badly wounded the editor of the *Whig*. In 1843 Hagan killed a man whose father he had attacked in his paper. In 1842 the *Sentinel* editor, now James F. Fall, nearly killed a banker named Robins, and two years later Robins scored his revenge by wounding another *Sentinel* editor, named Downs. Next, editor Hickey killed a Dr Macklin, and, some duels later, was himself killed duelling away from home in Texas. In 1845 Ryan, his successor, killed the editor of the *Whig* newspaper, and in 1848 Ryan was killed by a man who later bit the dust in his turn. It is said that journalists must have ink in their veins instead of blood: these men seem also to have had some itching powder that invisibly frayed their tempers.

(d) THE CHIEF CENTRES OF DUELLING

In the eighteen-fifties it was impossible to choose between half a dozen cities as the champion duelling-ground. Savannah, St Louis, Charleston, Natchez, Vicksburg, and New Orleans all had strong claims. That deadly pattern—pistols, ten paces, the undertaker—seems to have been traced almost daily.

New Orleans

The largest city in the South was New Orleans, and its large French population gave it a strong Latin flavour. Life there had a certain flamboyance: everybody behaved as extravagantly as the characters in a Dumas novel, full of windy talk about honour.

In such an atmosphere the duel was bound to flourish, the only difference from duels fought elsewhere being that the predominant weapon was the French one of the sword, and not the revolver. Rapiers and broadswords were much in demand, and the French fencing-masters made vast fortunes. Swords were less likely to be fatal than pistols, but when broadswords were used the result was sheer butchery.

The duel died very hard in New Orleans, and some were fought in the early nineteen-hundreds.

Centres of Duelling in the South and West

The wild gold diggers of California were not so wild that they did not stage duels as well as mere fights. The craze was at its height between 1850 and 1860, and in 1854 the little shanty town of San Francisco saw nine duels.

The rules too were just as rigorous as in the highly

civilized communities of Europe. For example, Judge Woodliff of Tennessee received a slap in the face from a drunken young man named Kewen. The onlookers stopped the Judge from killing his man on the spot. After sobering up, young Kewen said he would apologize publicly and privately. But according to the ' code of honour ' in Tennessee the rule was that no apology could wipe out a slap in the face, and naturally a judge must be a stickler for rules. Which was unlucky for Judge Woodliff, because in the subsequent duel the apologetic Kewen shot him dead.

It seemed that this sort of barbarous foolishness would go on for ever while the ' high-ups ' gave it such support. For example, J. W. Denver, Secretary of State, killed a Congressman in a duel—and has the capital of Colorado named after him.

But during the Civil War a change in public sentiment slowly began to show. In one of the hot-beds at least— South Carolina—one case killed duelling stone-dead. That was in 1878, when a lawyer named Shannon, who did not know the barrel of a revolver from the butt, was deliberately provoked to a duel by a Colonel Cash and pitilessly shot dead. That was too much. Not another duel was fought in South Carolina, but one death would not have had such an effect if public opinion had not changed. Possibly an earlier duel in 1859 also softened up public obstinacy when a husky but generous-minded gold-prospector and opponent of slavery was brutally killed in a duel by one of the Southern gentlemen. It was generally known that this duel was a put-up job to silence a troublesome opponent and therefore had nothing to do with the ' code of honour.'

" Satisfaction "

*A dramatic etching of an American
duel in about 1850*

Yet the tradition died hard in Virginia and Texas, and
the cowboy duel lasted well into this century. That form
of duel was part duel, part brawl. Any gentleman who
felt his honour besmirched by another would declare his
intention of shooting on sight. On meeting they would
walk towards each other, and as soon as one reached for
his gun the bullets would start to fly and the locals jump
for cover. Hundreds of films have exploited this situation, for the tension is real and dramatic. It is a duel at
high speed—no cool deliberation, no meeting of seconds,
but a split-second decision and lightning skill.

143

(e) END OF THE CODE

It is impossible to say why duelling reached such a pitch in the United States and why it lasted so long. Other countries had rough border regions; other countries had to fight against Nature and savages. Yet the duel was comparatively unknown in countries like Australia and New Zealand.

Whatever the reason, ridicule, as in England, did a great deal finally to kill the duel. Thus when two gentlemen of Louisville blazed away at each other in a street duel the newspapers made great play with the fact that they did not hurt each other, but did four hundred dollars' worth of damage to the shop-windows. And Mark Twain poked much fun at the duel in his *Autobiography*. He relates a duel in which he took part, but, although a Southerner, he burlesqued his own incompetence and the ' code of honour,' and did not hesitate to confess that he was terrified at the whole business. In *A Tramp Abroad* he ridiculed the French duel generally, and the Gambetta duel in particular. In *A Yankee at the Court of King Arthur* he laughed at the pseudo-medieval Walter Scott cult from which the American Southern duel had derived.

As with those other great laughter-makers, Rabelais and Cervantes, Mark Twain's humour did more than anything else to clear the air. Both State and Church had condemned duelling, but had been ineffectual against public opinion. But as soon as the young people read the great American humorist and saw how ridiculous their elders were as they strutted solemnly on their field of honour, then duelling was finished.

2

SOME FAMOUS AMERICAN DUELS

Alexander Hamilton and Aaron Burr (1804)

Perhaps the best-known of American duels is that which took place between Alexander Hamilton and Aaron Burr on July 11, 1804. Certainly the high rank of the contenders shows the grip duelling already exerted in the States.

Both men had served brilliantly in the war to free America from England, and Hamilton had afterwards won renown as a politician and economist. He had been Secretary of the Treasury under Washington, and on Washington's death he was appointed Commander-in-Chief of the American Army.

As for Aaron Burr, he was a leading politician who lost the Presidency of the United States to Jefferson in 1800 by only one vote. But Hamilton did not trust Burr, and it was through Hamilton's influence that Burr lost the Governorship of New York.

Burr was fighting mad, and looked for evidence to show that Hamilton had libelled him during this election campaign, so that he could issue a challenge.

The evidence came in a letter from a Dr Charles D. Cooper to Philip Schuyler, saying: " I assert that General Hamilton has declared in substance that they look upon Mr Burr as a dangerous man, not to be trusted. I could detail to you a still more despicable opinion which General Hamilton has expressed of Mr Burr."

At once Burr sent a second to challenge Hamilton, who was left in a quandary. He believed that he had done his duty, and he felt no personal enmity to Burr. Hamilton was also an opponent of duelling, having lost his eldest son, Philip, in a duel. He tried to hedge, but Burr would not let him, and in the end Hamilton reluctantly accepted.

Both men put their affairs in order, and it was plain that Hamilton feared the worst. It must have seemed ominous to him when they were rowed out to the duelling-ground at Weehawken Heights, off the Jersey shore of the Hudson river. It was on this same duelling-ground that his son had been killed.

Ten paces were marked out on that fine, fresh summer's morning, and Hamilton must have felt himself in the grip of a twice-repeated nightmare, for he knew that he did not intend to fire, but the grim look on Burr's face showed that he fully intended to kill his opponent.

The signal was given. Hamilton did not fire, but Burr fired only too accurately. Hamilton fell, shot in the right side: the former Secretary of the Treasury had been mortally wounded by the Vice-President of the United States.

After much suffering Hamilton died next day, his sorrowing wife, adopted daughter, and seven children at his bedside.

There was fierce indignation in the North against Burr, who showed no remorse. But he had to go into hiding for eleven days, after which he was smuggled to Philadelphia. From there he fled to seek the more congenial atmosphere of Georgia and Virginia. Despite the verdict at the coroner's inquest of wilful murder, Aaron Burr took his seat as President of the United States Senate.

A young clergyman, Lyman Beecher, was soon to preach a famous sermon against duelling, in which he did not mince words. He declared that the whole land was defiled with blood. " We act like a nation of murderers," he cried, " whilst we tolerate and even reward the perpetrators of the crime of duelling."

General Andrew Jackson ("Old Hickory") and Charles Dickinson (1806)

Tennessee was a very lawless border country, where men fought at the drop of a word, and " Old Hickory " was as explosive with words as he was with bullets. His opponent, Charles Dickinson, was just the sort of elegant young man to rile the old war-horse. That he was also the best shot in Tennessee did not deter " Old Hickory " for a moment.

A racehorse was the bone of contention, and the flow of epithets between them was so violent that apologies were unthinkable. The duel took place on May 22, 1806, on the Kentucky bank of the Red River north of Nashville, just outside the Tennessee state border.

This meant a full day's ride for the duellists, and Dickinson amused himself by showing off to his friends. The duel was to be fought at a distance of eight paces, instead of the normal ten, and at that distance Dickinson put four bullets into a silver dollar. He also severed pieces of string hanging from tavern doors. " Show those to General Jackson when he comes by! " he called to the tavern-keepers.

But General Jackson and his second, General Overton, did not need proof: they secretly believed that no man could hope to fight Dickinson and live. Jackson said, " Overton, I must hold my fire. I need more time than he does; I must have time to get a line on him." Overton shrugged. " Hickory, hold your fire, and it's a million to one you'll not be alive to fire! " " I know, but I'll take my chance of that; my luck's always good."

The arrangement was that the fighters should not face each other, but look at Overton. At the word, they were to turn and fire.

After the warning Overton called " Fire! " in a hurried manner, hoping that Dickinson's aim would be affected. Dickinson fired immediately at the gaunt, long form of " Old Hickory," dressed in his usual loose frock-coat. A puff of dust came from the left shoulder of that frock-coat. " Old Hickory " pressed his hand on the spot, but otherwise made no sign. Grimly he stood watching Dickinson, a crease on his leather cheeks that might have been a smile. " Great God, have I missed him? " cried Dickinson.

Then he realized that Jackson had not fired, and he stepped backward in panic.

" Back on your mark, sir! " called Overton, drawing his own pistol.

The white-faced Dickinson moved back to his mark, but he turned his head away, not caring to look death in the eyes.

Jackson was in no hurry. He wanted to spin out his moment of revenge for as long as possible, and Fate played into his hands. His pistol misfired and stopped at half-cock. That did not count under the rules, and poor

Dickinson had to endure that long agony of waiting once again. The bullet in his ribs must have come almost as a relief to him.

Overton walked across and looked at Dickinson. " He won't need any more from you, General," he announced.

Jackson nodded impassively, but as they walked away Overton noticed that Jackson's left shoe was full of blood.

" Jackson, are you hit? "

" Oh, I believe he has pinked me a little."

It turned out that Dickinson had not belied his reputation as a shot. He had tried for Jackson's heart, but he had not allowed for " Old Hickory's " scraggy body and his baggy frock-coat. The bullet had grazed the collarbone and broken a rib.

" Say nothing about it over there! " Jackson said, nodding towards the prostrate form of Dickinson, and the surgeons and seconds clustered around him.

To savour revenge to the full, Jackson wanted Dickinson, the best shot in Tennessee, to die in the belief that he had missed his man at eight paces. He got that revenge, for Dickinson could only lie in horrible pain, screaming curses at Jackson all day until death released him at eight in the evening.

It took " Old Hickory " a month to recover from his wound, but he summed it up himself when he said, " I should have hit him if he had shot me through the brain."

John Benton and Charles Lucas (1817)

This duel took place in Tennessee also, in 1817. Benton was a husky plainsman, while Lucas was a fine young lawyer and classical scholar, who, it was said, might one day aspire to be President of the United States.

Lucas accepted Benton's challenge, and proved his courage by taking Benton's bullet and firing into the ground himself.

But the thick-headed Benton was persuaded by malicious gossip to challenge Lucas again. By all the rules, Lucas need not have accepted, and at first he did decline the challenge.

But his own father, a judge, said that the " Lucas honour " demanded that his son should fight again. " Perhaps there is more in the Lucas honour than there is in common decency, in the fairness and in the good faith with which one civilized man should treat another," his son answered.

However, he accepted the challenge in the end, saying he must stand up like a fool and be shot down like a brute. Shot down he was, but what his father, the judge, thought as he looked down into the face of his dead son is not recorded.

The Unluckiest Officer in America : James Barron and Stephen Decatur (1820)

Possibly the unluckiest officer of all time was Commodore James Barron of the United States Navy. To be involved in one *cause célèbre* is normally enough to blight any man's career. But to be caught up in one just at the start of your career, to struggle for years against the effect, and then to be caught up in another would justify complaints from Job. Especially when you are a man of courage, patriotism, and an inventive ability that the young American nation much needed.

What finally blighted the career of Commodore Barron was the duel he fought with Commodore Stephen Decatur on March 22, 1820. His other trouble had occurred thirteen years before in 1807.

In that year England and the United States were officially at peace, but the British warship *Leopard* insisted on searching the American frigate *Chesapeake* off Virginia for British naval deserters.

In charge of the *Chesapeake* was Captain James Barron. Barron, aged thirty-nine, was considered one of the best officers in the service, and, as a good officer, he always obeyed orders. He had been instructed to avoid conflict with the British, and therefore when he had sighted the *Leopard* he had not cleared his decks for action, as that might have been considered provocative. But he reckoned without the ruthlessness of the British Navy.

Naturally, as the officer of a sovereign nation in his own home waters, Captain Barron refused the *Leopard's* demand. Without more ado, the *Leopard* opened fire on the *Chesapeake* at short range and continued the barrage for twenty minutes. Unprepared, the American frigate could fire only one shot before surrendering.

This caused a tremendous stir, and the American nation demanded war. That did not suit her rulers, and therefore somebody had to be sacrificed. It was Captain James Barron.

He was court-martialled for cowardice and weakness because he had not cleared for action. President Jefferson could have explained this, but he left this talented officer to his fate.

Barron was acquitted of cowardice, but found guilty on the other charge, and was sentenced to five years' suspension without pay. This meant, of course, his ruin. From that moment the epitaph " Barron of the *Chesapeake* " was always attached to his name.

But Barron struggled bravely for years in an obscure, poorly paid post in a merchant vessel. The head of the Navy Department, Commodore Stephen Decatur, firmly resisted all attempts to reinstate Barron.

Decatur was a dashing, handsome man and the petted idol of the nation, who saw in him their ideal of a seafaring hero. Decatur and Barron had been good friends, but Barron's ill-luck persisted. He had made a remark about Decatur's fiancée, not meant to be offensive, but Decatur had taken offence. He was never to forgive Barron for that unintended slight on his youthful pride.

Poor Barron struggled over the years without help, and all the time he saw Decatur thriving and refusing to give him a helping hand. Barron was an excellent inventor, but he could not even get the Navy Department to examine his ideas, which were twenty years in advance of his times. His only supporter was Captain Elliott, who had been a junior officer on the *Chesapeake*, and who was faithful, but unfortunately tactless.

Elliott heard that Decatur was openly sneering at Barron, and he passed this on. The goaded Barron having seen his family exist in poverty all those years could stand no more. He wrote to Decatur in 1819 asking if it was true that Decatur had said he could insult him as he liked. Decatur did not answer directly, but he knew how to sting Barron by insinuations.

Barron fell sick, possibly as a result of worry, but Decatur's attitude did not change. He was egged on against Barron by a Captain Bainbridge, and so, with

Elliott at Barron's elbow, many letters passed between them, culminating in a challenge to fight. With two Iagos whispering cunning words, what chance did either man have?

The duel was arranged to take place in Bladensburg on March 22, 1820.

Before firing, Barron, who had a fresh-complexioned, honest farmer's face, took a step towards his opponent. "Now, Decatur, if we meet in another world, let's hope that we may be better friends."

Decatur at once responded, "I never was your enemy."

The way was clear for the seconds to stop the fight. Honour would have been satisfied according to the rules, and no suspicion of cowardice could ever have stuck to Decatur in particular. But those two Iagos must see their play out.

"Gentlemen, to your places," Bainbridge called.

The two shots rang out, and both men fell. Decatur died, and Barron just escaped death. But the unfortunate fellow came back only to fresh opprobrium. After being dubbed "Barron of the *Chesapeake*" for so many years, for the rest of his life he was known as "the man who killed Decatur," and by that name he is still known.

The nation never forgave him for killing their hero, and it says much for human toughness that Barron lived to the age of eighty-two, and that the last years of his life were happy.

Henry Clay, Secretary of State, and Senator John Randolph of Virginia (1826)

Bragging accusations of lying uttered by politicians in

Congress often resulted in duels. This duel was one of these, and was fought on April 8, 1826. But the parties were reconciled, and the only damage was a bullet-pierced coat. Very different was the duel in 1838 between Jonathan Cilley and William Graves, the only one in which members of the House of Representatives were both principals and seconds. Cilley, the only New Englander to fight a duel, was killed by the first shot from his opponent's rifle.

The Black Knight of the South

As we have seen, duelling was most common in the South, and the attitude to duelling there is best summed up in the career of Colonel Alexander Keith McClung. McClung was a braggart, loafer, and bully, an exhibitionist who gloried in the title of " the Black Knight of the South." He was the best pistol-shot in the country, and he deliberately set out to live on that skill and do no useful work. He killed at least thirty people in duels, and his notorious career earned him a place in Mississippi's Hall of Fame, where his portrait can be seen to this day in the State Capitol at Jackson.

McClung was born in Kentucky in 1811, and from his first post as a midshipman at the Navy Yard in Brooklyn, New York, it was plain that he was a quarrelsome youth who intended to ride roughshod over anybody to whom he took a dislike. He fought several duels, but, almost for the only time, McClung's handsome face and polished manners failed to impress. His Captain rated him a quarrelsome, useless sailor, and he was dismissed.

McClung returned to Kentucky, and at once killed his first cousin, James Marshall, in a duel—or, as the phrase went, he ' took full satisfaction.' How many he killed at this time is not known, but in 1834 he deemed it wise to move to Mississippi on the pretence of studying law. He was described as an " exceedingly handsome young man with aristocratic tastes but no great financial resources, it being understood that he had run through his fortune."

It can readily be imagined that women ran after such a man—so handsome, so aristocratic, so inscrutable, and so deadly with a pistol. McClung enjoyed drinking, gambling, and free dinners, but it never occurred to him to work, either at law or anything else. He was born to grace the world for lesser mortals.

It appeared that John Menifee, of the Vicksburg Rifles, questioned this, and so found himself, rifle in hand, facing this handsome young stranger from Kentucky on Duelling Island in the Mississippi river.

The Regiment's officers turned out in force to see their companion send this civilian to the undertaker's. McClung showed no sign of fear, but continued to smoke until his adversary fired. As the ball whistled past, McClung threw his pipe away, walked calmly nearer, and shot his opponent dead. McClung melodramatically kissed his rifle and thanked God for having directed his bullet exactly. At which the ladies no doubt decided that McClung was modest as well as brave, clever, and handsome.

Six Menifees still lived, and these, one after the other, challenged McClung to fight, and one after the other McClung killed them.

Let us hope that the Menifee women were satisfied that their menfolk had satisfactorily guarded the family honour. What is certain is that from then on McClung was a legend. He was known as " The Black Knight of the South " because he always appeared on the duelling-ground in black clothes. That legend became stronger when he shot another young man in a duel at a distance of a hundred feet. McClung said he would hit his opponent " in the teeth," and that's exactly what he did. It has been called the most remarkable shot with a smooth-bore pistol in the whole history of duelling.

The record of killings went on, for McClung's heavy drinking seems not to have affected his aim. But McClung never did anything but kill. He fought well in the Mexican War, for his physical courage was unquestionable, and, having the gift of the gab, he tried to get into Congress, but was defeated. McClung continued to sponge on everybody he met, but at last he reached a point where he owed money everywhere and none of his friends wanted to know him.

On March 23, 1855, McClung fired his pistol for the last time, and kept his record of never missing. But this was his easiest target: he shot himself.

CONCLUSION

In 1868, six years after an Englishman last fought a duel, a writer was able to say that " No arguments are required to demonstrate the wickedness and absurdity of duelling."

There is not much fault to be found with that statement. Duels were wicked, and they were absurd, but we must never forget that we are looking back. It is easy to condemn and oversimplify the actions of people who lived long ago. If any of us had lived a hundred and fifty years ago, can we be sure that we should have had the courage to refuse to fight if our ' honour ' had been challenged? It needs imagination and independence to go against the swim, and there is a blind instinct which tells us to fight when our personal pride is hurt. Moreover, men have always believed that by being prepared to die—and, one may add, to kill—they will convince others that what they die for is right. So none of us can be sure that we should not have found ourselves squinting down a pistol-barrel or flashing a sword in the cold morning air.

You may believe that we have ' risen above ' that sort of thing now, but once again the question is, can we be sure?

In the early years of this century duelling became a

regular feature of German university life. There were societies devoted to its cult, and it became a social stigma to refuse a challenge. Deaths were not infrequent. Duelling was supposed to show manliness, and although most authorities condemned the practice, it did not lack some support, even among the learned. An American professor said, " Duelling, it must be admitted, is an evil in the universities. But there are others equally great and much meaner. . . . The German system, although brutal, is manly. It holds the student to the strictest account for all he does and says. The rapier puts all men on an equal footing. . . ."

The historian of the German universities, Paulsen, sees that this is untrue, but even he says that the exuberance of youth will out, and duelling is not the worst way to express it.

At any rate, even in the present century, the custom of duelling persisted in the German universities throughout the nineteen-twenties and was encouraged under the Nazi Government of Hitler. If duels were supposed to indicate manliness, and if they were " Affairs of honour upon which neither reason nor morals have any right to sit in judgment," then obviously Hitler, glib exponent of illogicalities, would be sure to seize on duels eagerly.

You may say that these modern examples of duelling come only from a nation always ready to be dazzled by the soap-bubbles of military vainglory. But let us never forget that although we do not fight single duels, man to man, we fight, and are always making ready to fight, terrible wars, nation against nation. All that has been said against duelling can be said against war. When nations quarrel and go to war to ' settle the argument ' they are being just as nonsensical as the gentleman next to St Foix in the eighteenth-century coffee-house.

It is also interesting to note that all the arguments so strangely put forward in favour of duelling have also been used in support of war.

It used to be argued

1. That duelling was a means devised by Nature to check the too rapid increase of the population.
2. That duelling keeps bullies in check. (There might be something in this but for the fact that there is no reason why a bully should not be a fine swordsman or pistol-shot.)
3. That if men could not resent injuries openly by fighting with deadly weapons they would use those weapons secretly.
4. That duelling was in the nature of mankind, and nothing would ever get rid of it.
5. That duelling makes people conduct themselves with good manners.

Duelling and warfare are also alike in that they both often cause men to display great courage and devotion to a belief. But men and women will produce those qualities in whatever situation they are in. They stem from Nature, and do not need the threat of a senseless death to bring them out. More often, the worst qualities in mankind are aroused by war.

At one time Greenlanders had a more practical way of settling private quarrels. They did not use knives, pistols, or swords to settle disputes. Each man composed a poem making game of his opponent, and then he sang this poem in public, accompanied by his friends as chorus. The winner was the man who got the most laughs.

And, in the end, it is possibly the absurdity and wastefulness of war that are the strongest arguments against it, although we now have a practical argument that would appear to be unanswerable—the hydrogen bomb. It would seem that the choice is plain: mankind must either get rid of war or the extinction of humanity will follow.

But man has kept his nose above water for a long, long time, and the day will surely come when the slaughter of war between nations will be as old-fashioned as the slaughter of duelling between individuals.

INDEX

INDEX

Field of the Cloth of Gold, the, 34
Fisher, James, 11, 26–27
Fitzgerald, Thomas (Prior of the Knights of St John), 52
Fox, Charles James, 57, 86–88, 105
Francis I, King of France, 58
Franklin, Benjamin, ix, 130
Frizell, Mr, 103–104
Fullarton, Colonel, 88–90, 92, 97

GAMBETTA, LÉON, 123, 144
Garrick, George, 82–84
Gaston of Béarn, 30
Gastonois, the Count of, 14
Gastonois, the Countess of, 14–15
George III, 61, 97, 131
Georgia, 132, 147
Gilbert and Sullivan, operas of, 120
Gilbert the Goose, 21
Glassonby, Manor of, 21
Gloucester Lodge, Brompton, 115
Godwine of Winchester, 19
Gontran, 14–16
Gordon, General, 95
Gould, the Hon. Mr Justice, 91
Gower, Mr, 71–73
Graham, Mr, 103
Grammont-Cadérousse, Duc de, 121
Greenlanders, 159
Gubuin, Ralph (Prior of Tynemouth), 12
Gundobad, King of Burgundy, 1–3

HAGAN (editor of the *Sentinel*), 140
Haig, Captain, 101–102
Halidon Hill, battle of, 35
Haly, Dr, 131
Hamilton, Alexander, 145–146
Hampstead Heath, 59
Hanson, Captain, 90–91
Harty, Isle of, 28
Hawke, Martin Bladen, second Baron, 105
Hawkslaw, manor of, 21
Henrietta Maria, Queen, 65
Henrietta Street, Covent Garden, 85
Henry I, 9
Henry II, 4, 9, 11, 19
Henry III, 4
Henry IV, King of England, 50, 51
Henry IV, King of France, 58

Henry VI, 52–53
Henry VII, 54
Henry VIII, 34
Henry, Duke of Hereford, 48–50
Henry, Duke of Lancaster, 36
Herbert, Edward, first Baron of Cherbury, 59
Hervey, Lord, 73–74
Hickey (editor of the *Sentinel*), 140
Hillas, Major, 116–117
Hitler, Adolf, 158
Holland House, Kensington, 110
Hood, Samuel, first Viscount, 108
Hotham, William, first Baron, 108
Howard, Colonel, 64
Hudson, Jeffery, 65–66
Hudson river, 134
Humberstone, Major, 87
Hyde Park, 75, 87, 88, 104, 106

INGELGER, COUNT OF ANJOU, 15–16
Ireton, Henry, 59

JACKSON, ANDREW (" Old Hickory "), 147–149
Jackson, Major James, 132–133
Jackson, President, 135
James I, 59, 63
Jamestown, 131
Janin, Jules, 122
Jarnac, the Chevalier de, 58
Jefferson, President, 145
Jermyn, Mr, 64
John, King, 20
Juliers, 64
Julius, Mr, 103

KATRINGTON, THOMAS, 38–42
Kensington, 92
Kensington Gravel Pits, 67
Kentucky, 154, 155
Keon, Mr Robert, 96, 111
Kerbogha, Emir of Mosul, 1
Kerr, General, 112
Kewen, 142
Kilburn Wells, 105
Kilmaurs, Lord, 76–78
King's College, London, 119
Kingsdown, 85
Kingston Assizes, 91
Kinloss, Edward Bruce, Lord, 64
Knightsbridge Barracks, 104

163